THE NEXUS DAYS

The Golden Age of Black Nightlife in New Orleans

KARIN G. HOPKINS

Foreword by Noah Hopkins

ISBN: 978-0-578-88419-6
First Printing June 2021

Library of Congress Control Number: 2021938933

Front Cover Design:
Malcolm Edgecombe of ME Design Solutions

Back Cover Design:
Malcolm Edgecombe & Noah Hopkins

Multimedia Marketing Services: Jackson Squared Media

Interior Design: Jessica Tilles of TWA Solutions & Services

From the Author:
This book is a compilation of my own memories as well as
recollections from other people that I interviewed. In a few
instances, in order to maintain their anonymity, I chose not to
name individuals. I have formatted some experiences into quoted
dialog. Also, some incidents are fictionalized, written in context
to the times and circumstances.

Printed in the United States of America

"I've learned that people will forget what you said, people will forget what you did, but people will never forget how you made them feel."

—Maya Angelou

Table of Contents

FOREWORD

I am a big guy, but I don't have a big head. Now, if you think I'm talking about my hat size, you're missing the point. When I deny being big-headed, I mean I do not have a big ego. That's why it's weird to hear someone describe me as a "Renaissance Man." But I get it. NEXUS, the nightclub that has become my signature success story, shaped this perception. Co-owned by me and Richard Powell, NEXUS was a popular nightclub in New Orleans in the 1980s. If Studio 54 and the Cotton Club had conceived a baby, they would have birthed NEXUS.

NEXUS was two clubs under one roof—up-tempo dance music upstairs and live jazz downstairs. It was a place of enjoyment, yet it was also a business operation that ran like a well-oiled machine.

Somehow, the NEXUS leadership chose the exact right people for services and management. That's how NEXUS became a place where administrative structure and creative innovation easily co-existed.

The backstory to NEXUS starts with me, Noah Hopkins, known as a child by my nickname "Butch" when I grew up in inner-city New Orleans. Surrounded by urban decay and subjected to low expectations, how did I transcend these challenges? Big dreams. Hard work. Long hours. Lady Luck. Divine grace. All of that plus a really good family.

I had six sisters—Sylvia, Elaine, Fern, Toni, Naomi, and Sherry. I also had four brothers—Lionel, Bruce, Don, and Claude. Including me, that's eleven children. My parents did the best they could considering the hardships they had to bear.

My mother stayed home and raised us, so my father worked many jobs. With no training in anything specific, he took any job he could get. He was mostly a truck driver, as I remember. He drove 18-wheelers and delivery trucks for a drug store chain called K&B (Katz & Besthoff). As a child, the one thing I remember about my father is that he went to work, in sickness and bad weather; that man went to work and never complained. I guess I couldn't appreciate what he did until I became an adult.

Thinking back to when my sisters, brothers, and I were kids, I see how selfish we were. Speaking for myself, I didn't understand why we didn't get toys or new clothes for holidays like other children. I couldn't see that our parents were making sacrifices and concentrating on real priorities—food on our plates and a roof over our heads. They knew these necessities were way more important than things that would break or wear out, eventually.

If my mother had been born in today's era and had she been white, she would have become a great artist. Her handwriting was like fine calligraphy. She did pen and ink drawings and etchings. She was a very talented artist. In hindsight, I must acknowledge I got my work ethics from my father and my art skills from my mother. They are both deceased now.

Sometimes, when I think about what they did for me and my siblings, I get angry with myself for whining when I was a child and not being able to see that we were better off than many other children. We had both of our parents and they were excellent role models.

When Karin came to me and said she wanted to write a book about *The NEXUS Days* and trace the story back to my childhood, I said no. Even though people see me as an outgoing person, I am very private. I am not comfortable sharing my personal business. Besides, being poor is nothing to brag about and as a child, my family had just enough to survive. Karin helped me to reframe my attitude. We didn't have money, but my family was rich in other ways. Our parents taught us right from wrong. We had to go to school and strive for good grades. We had to use soap, water, and toothpaste. We had to share. We laughed a lot. Most importantly, we received unconditional love.

We grew up in Gert Town on a street named Mars Place. Our neighborhood consisted of other poor families that city folks would call "country" but everybody had a good heart.

If NOPSI (New Orleans Public Service Inc.) cut off somebody's power, a neighbor would create an emergency hook up by stringing an extension cord between the two houses. My momma used to say, "It would be a shame for them to lose what little food they had in their refrigerator."

Through Facebook, I have reconnected with old friends from my childhood neighborhoods, including Ernette Sterling and Mildred Toney (Collier).

Ernette made me remember that her grandfather was a barber, with a shop in the family's backyard. I also recall another neighborhood barber named Sam Green. These businessmen modeled entrepreneurial risk-taking and self-sufficiency, unaware that as they were cutting my hair, they also were shaping my future.

Mildred recalled the good times she shared with my sister, Fern, and how everyone cared for each other when we were growing up. I don't know if it was like this throughout New Orleans back then, but that's what we saw when we were children. It was compassion and empathy from people who had little, but willingly shared much.

The most famous name in Gert Town isn't a person, it's an institution—Xavier University. As you read the book, you'll see the role this school played in my life, even though I was not a student at Xavier. Gert Town also produced many incredible people, especially entertainers.

The father of jazz, Buddy Bolden, was from Gert Town. He mixed ragtime, blues, gospel, and brass band into a new sound, which eventually became jazz. Bunk Johnson played the trumpet with Buddy Bolden's band and many other shows that toured nationally. Allen Toussaint was a legendary songwriter, producer, and arranger. Toussaint's name is on hundreds of hit songs from the 1960s through the 2000s. Red Tyler was a sax player who played R&B but considered himself a jazzman.

Tami Lynn was a versatile vocalist who was an opening act for many jazz greats, recorded with R&B musicians and performed backup for the best recording artists in the business. Merry Clayton performed a duet with Mick Jagger and also sang with other superstar entertainers. She is an actress with credits in major movies and Broadway shows. Garrett Morris is an actor and comic who was an original member of the *Saturday Night Live* cast. Everywhere these amazing people went, Gert Town's talent was on display.

Karin saw all of these influences: devoted parents, business owners, and outstanding artists as the foundation of self-esteem, confidence, compassion, and resilience. I can't argue with her.

I'm telling you about my childhood, so you can see how I gradually moved up in life. I owe my successes to a bunch of people, some related to me by blood, others related by community kinship.

My childhood gave me everything I needed to conquer the world. Eventually, I had a change of heart and supported the book. I even wrote this Foreword section to enhance

Karin's efforts. She is my wife and she has always been in my corner, so as her husband, I chose to reciprocate. Since she was passionate about this, I got on board.

She has laid our lives bare, sharing our hurts and healings, shame and redemption, bad breaks and comebacks.

There are lessons in these pages for people who suffered as children, yearn for love, are working to sustain a marriage, aspire to create a business, and dream of running a nightclub. There is even a look at the inner workings of TV news.

Before I conceded, Karin had done a lot of research, starting with pictures of The Exchequer and NEXUS in our photo albums. It is a blessing we still have these pictures. Karin also compiled a list of people associated with both clubs and reached out to many of them for interviews. Being a former reporter, research comes naturally to her. And since she is a technology geek, she easily cruises the Internet and social media platforms.

She started by asking me a lot of questions like: How did I know what business to open? Who was involved with me in this project and that business deal? How did I attract the funds to get started? How did I decide on a name? What factors determine a good location?

This project was on her heart and in her spirit, that's where it began and now *The NEXUS Days* is a book that I hope becomes a bestseller.

If you know me well, you have heard me say, "*God has always put good people in my life,*" and I am saying with sincere admiration that Sidney Richmond was truly a good human being and so is Richard Powell. At separate times, we partnered on club projects. Before NEXUS and Richard, there were The Exchequer and Sidney.

I met Sidney around 1978 at a New Orleans National Business League meeting, which was a chapter of the National Business League (NBL). The NBL was founded by Booker T. Washington in 1900. I was president of the local chapter and would have a networking session before the meeting got started.

I also hung around a little after the meeting to network. Having similar goals, Sidney and I became fast friends. He was a medical technician at Charity Hospital, and I was a sales representative for Metropolitan Life insurance. We often spoke about doing something other than a regular job, but neither of us could afford to quit working. So, we kept our jobs to pay our bills. But as we thought about the possibilities, we made a commitment.

Whatever we did, it had to be something that would make a lot of money. You will learn later in the book how these conversations led to The Exchequer, which was the club Sidney and I opened in 1979. Why am I mentioning The Exchequer? Because it was like the successful big brother to NEXUS.

Richard Powell attended Pharmacy School at Xavier University and I was in school at Southern University of New Orleans (SUNO). My then-girlfriend was also at Xavier

University in the School of Pharmacy, so I spent a lot of time on Xavier's campus and made many friends, often playing flag football with some of the guys. Even after everyone graduated, some fellas I played football with formed an alumni team and invited me to play with them. Richard played on the alumni team and we became friends.

I think of those days and recall the players whose names I can remember—Raymond Dever, Bobby Johnson, Michael Ingersoll, Ronald Thomas (our quarterback), and Richard Powell. Those were some fun Saturdays. There were a lot of other guys, too, but my memory has never been good, and it's gotten worse with age. We all went on to the next phase in life. Richard moved to Chicago and opened a pharmacy. I had settled into a comfortable job as a medical sales representative for Mead-Johnson Laboratories. Later, Richard and I became business partners in NEXUS.

When Richard and I collaborated on the NEXUS project, we knew what kind of club we wanted. It had to be first class, upscale, safe, and well managed. To do it right, we knew it would take working capital (a fancy term for start-up money). Richard had the initial investment. Together, we came up with the name NEXUS (meaning "the connection"). I had the nightclub IQ and oversaw the renovation and construction phase and made decisions concerning design, color scheme, hiring personnel, stocking the two bars, and promotions.

Richard and I knew his investment alone would not allow us to accomplish all of this, so he introduced me to another guy from Chicago, who brought in a friend of his from Atlanta. Their money took us to the next level with Richard and me as managing partners of the business. Things didn't work out with the other partners, so we quickly bought them out, leaving Richard and me as co-owners and general managers of one of the most successful clubs in New Orleans history.

NEXUS was a very special place for professionals and everyone else who came to the club. No customer was better than any other customer. NEXUS treated everyone with respect. NEXUS was always about customer service and building relationships. Today, the word for this is "branding."

Although Richard Powell and Noah Hopkins created this venue for our customers, we couldn't do it by ourselves. We hired the right managers: Keith Whitehead, George Williams, Terry Davis, and Don Spears. Our go-to man for special projects was Chris Smith.

Our downstairs jazz musicians were David Torkanowky, Chris Severin, and Julian Garcia. NEXUS had talented deejays for the upstairs dance crowd—LeBron Joseph, A.D. Berry, Slick Leo, Daryl George, and Eric Sterling. Our frontline staff—bartenders, waiters, and bar porters—provided great service.

We had off-duty New Orleans Police Department (NOPD) security details that kept us safe: Farrell St. Martin, Clarence Taplin, Leroy St. Martin, Romalis Stukes, and Malcolm Williams. I considered Harry Williams to be my personal security. A reserve New Orleans police officer, Harry, became a trusted ally and close friend. We had an efficient administrative assistant, Lisa Ross. I must acknowledge the man who kept the building smelling clean and fresh, Lawrence Gilbert. I thank all the people named above, and I hope the people I forgot will forgive me. However, the people I thank and appreciate most are the LOYAL NEXUS CUSTOMERS.

We had celebrities at NEXUS, big events, and excitement every time the doors were open. Considering all the great things that happened there, one thing stands out—the customer who had me from the moment she said hello. Karin Lynn Grant (Hopkins) has been my better half. She got me to see my life through fresh eyes, and she wrote this book. I thank her for the investment of time and talent. She truly is my pride and joy.

Love you, honey!

Noah Hopkins lives in Tuskegee, Alabama, and works as a consultant to individuals, organizations, towns, and cities on business development and tourism commerce projects.

PREFACE

by Karin Hopkins

W hen I answered the phone, I had no idea the call would transform my life. Kristian Newman, one of my closest sister-friends, asked me if I knew Master P.

"I have never met him, but I certainly know who he is," I answered.

Master P is a big shot in the music industry. He started as a street hustler in New Orleans, then went legit as a record store owner in Richmond, California. He returned to New Orleans with a no-limits attitude and cultivated a stable of talented artists into recording hit-makers and rambunctious money-makers.

So yes, I knew his background. But why had she asked the question?

While watching a television docuseries about Master P on a national cable network, his life story fascinated her. Then she heard something that set her hair on fire.

He met his wife at NEXUS.

NEXUS was a nightclub in New Orleans, famous for match-making in the realms of finance and romance.

NEXUS is the reason I have written this book, which is ultimately a tribute to the man who was the heart and soul of the NEXUS era.

Former customers who boogied down, hooked up, networked, and hung out still talk about the experience he created.

That was then, and this is now; a time for remembering *The NEXUS Days.*

1

Fate is a Real Mother For Ya

L to R: Noah Hopkins, Lambert Boissiere, Jr., and Horace Jones

His story begins at his pinnacle, at least by his standards. He thought he had everything—success, money, fancy cars, a wife, side chick, and lots of one-night stands. His life couldn't get any better. But one evening, with a full moon hanging in a velvet sky, a woman walked into his world and his wild ways instantly ended.

From his new beginning to his life now, I know his story well because it is my story, too.

My name was Karin Grant, and I spent many years in television news, rising to the coveted spot of news anchor.

When I accepted an offer at a TV station in New Orleans, I crossed paths with Noah Hopkins. I remember the exact date we met—October 11, 1985. Since details like this are not his strong suit, he trusts my memory.

We both recall our introduction at NEXUS, the two-story club he established on Elysian Fields in a blue-collar neighborhood near the lakefront in New Orleans.

It was a busy Friday night with a packed house, yet we were in an imaginary bubble—talking, laughing, and beginning a journey, mapped out by the hand of fate.

That night and everything that led up to it often replays in my head like a favorite movie that never gets old.

2

Do You Know What It Means to Explore New Orleans?

"**W**e have two and three-bedroom units," said the leasing agent at the luxury apartment building I had visited when I was scouting places to live in New Orleans. Her description of the amenities closed the deal. "We have twenty-four-hour guard service, spacious entrance lobby with a sweeping staircase, gated entrance to the parking garage, assigned parking spaces for each tenant, a landscaped courtyard, and rooftop terrace."

1750 St. Charles Avenue was high-priced living, with many high-profile tenants. Often, when the elevator doors would open, the person standing inside the elevator cage would be the notorious yet charismatic Louisiana governor, Edwin Edwards. I was never sure whether he was visiting someone with an apartment in the building or if he was my neighbor.

As a New Orleans journalist, I covered many stories involving Governor Edwards, including several scandals.

You can imagine how tempting it was to go for a news scoop when we were both riding an elevator. If it had been just the governor and me, perhaps I would have. However, the two big, gun-toting bodyguards protecting him were intimidating. To be honest, that's not really why I held back.

In this building, everyone respected each other's privacy. Besides, it was easy to score an interview with Edwards going through normal channels.

In the 1970s and 1980s, Edwards was the bad boy of Louisiana politics who seemingly threw up his middle finger at federal prosecutors. He was quick and slick with his words, too. In 1983, he bragged that the only way he could lose an election was if someone caught him in bed "with a dead girl or a live boy."

Federal prosecutors tried time after time to bust Edwards, but he was like Teflon; they would hit him with charges, and nothing would stick. Eventually, however, his luck ran out. The feds flipped someone the governor knew and trusted into a Judas. This man was not only a friend, but he was also a contractor hired by Edwards to build the governor's house in Baton Rouge. While the work was being done, this friend installed listening devices on Edwards's home phone system and inside his house. Not knowing he was being recorded, Edwards talked freely in the privacy of his home and the feds picked up juicy evidence.

Intriguing stories like this made my job beyond fascinating. I covered everything from flamboyant politicians like Edwin Edwards to free spirits like Ruthie the Duck Lady, and every day was an adventure.

When I first started at WVUE Channel 8, I worked the early morning shift, meaning I had to be at my desk before daybreak. It was a tough grind but I loved my workday ritual; hopping out of bed during morning darkness, choosing my wardrobe for that day, applying my makeup, styling my hair, greeting the doormen as I headed to the parking garage, sliding into my dark blue Mercedes Benz for the drive from my apartment to the TV station, reviewing the previous night's news scripts, pulling stories from national and international news agencies e.g. Reuters, U.P.I. (United Press International) and A.P. (Associated Press), reading *The Times Picayune* newspaper, monitoring the police scanner, grabbing a stack of script paper and pounding the keys on my typewriter to compose a series of news stories that would be fresh for the early morning audience.

I left work usually about two o'clock in the afternoon, and since I had no friends in New Orleans, I explored the city.

My neighborhood was a mixture of obvious affluence and obscene poverty.

Lining St. Charles Avenue were massive oak trees, many dripping with brightly colored Mardi Gras beads, adding a touch of humor to this refined street dominated by elegant mansions. These monuments to wealth looked to me like castles in a fairy tale.

Venturing across St. Charles Avenue, into neighborhoods just a few blocks away, morphed the fairy tale into a scary tale with abandoned businesses, run-down houses, prostitution, drug dealing, and other signs of decline, deprivation, and despair. I would soon learn that it wasn't just streets like Melpomene and Dryades that were dangerous.

Learning New Orleans was now my job. So, I paid close attention during morning meetings. That is where reporters would pitch their ideas or get told what stories they would be covering.

The American Nutrition Association was holding a convention in New Orleans, and the weekday assignment editor dispatched me there. "Make sure you go in with open eyes and get at least two angles out of that convention. We need different slants for the five and ten o'clock newscasts."

With the news truck loaded up with gear—Ikegami camera, tripod, cables, battery case with fully charged batteries, clip-on and handheld microphones with WVUE logo cuffs and mike stands for desktop interviews—it was time to go to work. Paired with my favorite photographer, Lloyd Edwards, the day was starting just fine. Lloyd cranked up the news van and I hopped in the passenger seat, pushing the button that turned on the radio, pre-set to WYLD FM 98.5.

We pulled out of the WVUE Channel 8 garage onto Jefferson Davis Parkway, turned onto Earhart Boulevard, and drove downtown, headed to the convention center.

WYLD FM 98.5 had kept us entertained during the drive. With the song on the radio coming to an end, the deejay took over the airwaves, expertly turning a knob on his control board to raise the volume of his voice, then turning another knob to lower the music for a smooth fade out.

Arriving at the convention center, I pushed the button, turning off the radio, grabbed my reporter's notebook, checked the mirror, and bounced out of the news truck. Lloyd unloaded his equipment as I walked into the convention center to find the event coordinator.

"You can set up your cameras against this backdrop and I will get the president of our organization to meet you here for an interview." This was a standard comment from an event liaison not authorized to act as a spokesperson.

Lloyd mounted his state-of-the-art camera onto a tripod and also attached a handheld microphone. "Karin, we need a mike check."

"Mary had a little lamb...whose fleece was white as snow...and everywhere that Mary went...the lamb was sure to go..."

Reciting this little nursery rhyme was my way of giving the cameraman sound to adjust the audio volume to my voice level.

Within minutes, the liaison returned, along with the organization's president.

Shoulders back, microphone thrust forward, I began the interview, hoping to get a good soundbite with my first question.

"What is the theme for the convention?"

"Our theme this year aligns with the federal government's dietary recommendations and how they have changed over time."

Next question.

"Being that you're in New Orleans, where nutrition is not usually on the menu or the dinner plate, what do you say to local residents about our eating habits?"

"In no way are we telling people to clean out their refrigerators and cabinets and purge themselves of the great tasting foods that are such New Orleans traditions. We do recommend a modified way of seasoning and cooking those dishes that satisfies the palate and also promotes good health."

After the interview, we went into the exhibit hall to get B-roll footage of cooking demonstrations, vendors, and crowds.

With my main story written in my reporter's notebook, I decided on the angle for a simpler version that would become a V/O. This is the abbreviation for a voice-over, which is the news anchor looking into the camera, reading words that explain what the audience is seeing on their TV screens.

We left the convention center to go speak with random people on the street about food issues.

I wanted to know whether people would change their recipes to fit the more nutritious recommendations discussed during the interview at the convention center.

We drove to the French Quarter and approached a man on Royal Street who somewhat resembled the famous chef, Paul Prudhomme.

"I know you. You're that girl on TV, Karin Grant."

"Yes, sir. Thank you so much for watching me and even remembering my name. I'd like to interview you for the news tonight about your food choices and how those decisions affect your weight. May I ask your name?"

"My name is Ono Dunlap."

"Would you spell that please?"

"If I say it real clear, bet you can figger out how to spell it."

"Okay, I'm listening."

The man grabbed his head and shouted, "Oh no, my belly done lapped over my belt."

I lost it. My composure crumbled. I laughed so hard my stomach ached.

We gathered a few more Man-On-The-Street interviews, which for my principles had to include women. With our scheduled work done, we shut down for lunch, visiting Lloyd's mother on Baronne Street. It was Monday and in New Orleans that meant red beans and rice. I had developed a love for this thick, creamy comfort food. In my kitchen, however, a can of Blue Runner Red Beans was a convenient shortcut. Her beans were slow-cooked, seasoned with a ham bone and andouille sausage. This slice of home-cooked heaven became a weekly ritual. Along with devouring a great meal, I got a peek inside Lloyd's life. These lunches solidified our dynamic duo chemistry. They triggered an endorphin release, making everything easy, including returning to work to finish the day's assignment.

First stop—a recording booth, which is a small space with padded walls where I read my scripts into a recording machine. Lloyd moved to another room with two tapes, one containing raw B-roll video recorded in the field. The other tape was the master for the packaged report.

Lloyd transferred my recorded voice track onto the master and then meticulously built a finished story to air on the evening news.

Packaged stories, which usually were under two minutes in total running time, were the hardest and most time-consuming to edit. I had taken notes in the field that were critical to efficient editing.

I had the exact time codes showing where the soundbites were on the raw tapes as well as the soundbite incues and outcues. Anchor voice-overs were usually thirty to forty-five seconds and required less editing time. Completed, we would label the tapes and have them delivered to the control room. There were different versions for the 5:00 p.m. and 10:00 p.m. newscasts.

Times had changed since my career first began. A TV station in Detroit hired me immediately after I graduated from Wayne State University with a degree in Mass Communications. Back then, we shot the news on film and passed it to others for processing, which was a slow, tedious process.

A revolution transformed news photography in the 1970s with electronic news-gathering (ENG) equipment, followed by 3/4-inch tapes that reduced editing from hours to minutes, and then Beta tapes hit the scene. Reflecting on this reminds me of the progression of my professional journey.

After several years in Texas, I moved to New Orleans in August 1985, where I developed a daily ritual. After work, I would go home and change clothes for my afternoon stroll around town.

Once, while I was walking along Rampart Street, two men suddenly appeared and struck up a conversation. I saw it as a friendly overture until I learned where they had been the last ten years.

"We just got out of Angola," the Charles Manson lookalike told me as he and his cross-eyed Black buddy closed in.

Angels in heaven must have been looking out for me. Intuitively, I knew I was in the presence of evil, but inexplicably, I was not harmed.

Another time, I was walking in the Lower French Quarter when a man approached me and confessed he had been following me for blocks. He said he thought I was a queen.

Naïve as a tourist from Topeka, my mind conjured up images of an Ancient Egyptian Empire—exquisite textiles, jewelry, and symbols adorning the ruling class in pre-colonial Africa contrasted with my appearance at that moment. Perplexed, I thought, *Wearing jeans and a T-shirt, how can he think I am African royalty?"*

Later I was told that I had been in the gay part of New Orleans, where "queen" had a definition of its own.

These walks gave me something to do with my alone time.

But one fateful day, someone invited me to a happy hour and my days of solitary wandering would soon be over.

3

History Lived at NEXUS

Jezelle Hebert was a beautiful Creole who knew my friend, Rosemary "Cookie" Rylander, from their days in Lafayette, Louisiana. I had met Cookie when she was a social worker and I was a TV reporter in Beaumont, Texas.

Cookie shared my contact information with Jezelle and after a few conversations, we agreed to a girls' night out. On a Friday evening, we drove into areas of New Orleans that were completely new to me.

Approaching the corner of Elysian Fields Avenue and Robert E. Lee Boulevard, I wondered about the historical references. The Elysian Fields occupy a special place in Greek mythology, and Robert E. Lee was a Confederate general in the Civil War.

Those thoughts quickly left my mind as we got closer to our destination.

I felt like Dorothy discovering the Emerald City. Glowing with bright lights and brimming with people who put the happy in the hour, NEXUS was nightclub nirvana. This place was popping like Black nightclubs in New York that operated between 1920 and 1940, including one that is etched in infamy.

From books and pictures, I knew about the Cotton Club, but I was more impressed by Minton's Playhouse.

Founded in the late 1930s by a tenor saxophonist, this nightclub was a second home for Black jazz musicians, a place where they could play their music and socially rub elbows.

The owner, Henry Minton, was more than a talented musician. He was also the first-ever Black delegate to the largest musician's union in the world. Minton had business skills, too, which was evident when he served as the manager of the Rhythm Club in Harlem. All of this gave Minton an insider's perspective of the economics of running a business and the preferences of jazz musicians in New York.

Destined to succeed, when he opened Minton's in 1938, he had laid the groundwork through his relationships in the jazz community.

For many years, Minton's was the epicenter of live jazz performances. The maestros of the day played there, including Miles Davis, Thelonious Monk, Charlie Parker, and Dizzy Gillespie. The First Ladies of Song and the Gentlemen of Jazz also graced the stage at Minton's, including Ella Fitzgerald, Sarah Vaughan, Duke Ellington, and Louis Armstrong.

Whereas Minton's was good *for* Black music and good *to* Black musicians, the Cotton Club was a different story.

Opened in 1923, the Cotton Club profited from Black talent and provided steady income to Black musicians and dancers.

Truthfully, the Cotton Club was another plantation with a contemporary slave master.

Owned by a bootlegger, gangster, and convicted felon named Owney Madden, the Cotton Club was a place where people could get liquor during the prohibition era when the 18th Amendment to the US Constitution outlawed booze.

Featuring top quality entertainers, the Cotton Club also perpetuated racist stereotypes.

Images depicted Black people as savages in the jungle or slaves on Southern plantations, and portrayed Black women in ways that were racist and misogynistic.

The Cotton Club, however, had some redeeming factors. Entry was expensive for the white customers. With their money filling his pockets, Owney Madden had plenty of cash, and despite his racist attitude, he paid Black performers top dollar.

Just as he hired Black musicians, he also appreciated the beauty of Black women, hiring them as chorus girls.

The Cotton Club advertised for "tall, tan, and terrific" Black women, at least five-feet-six in height, light-skinned, and under twenty-one years of age.

Black entertainers were forbidden to mix with the club's clientele, forcing them to find alternative options after performances. Often that meant a friendly basement where they were free to drink and socialize.

Noah captured the best of both establishments in NEXUS, which he opened in 1983.

He liked NEXUS, but he loved the business he created before this. The model and inspiration for NEXUS was The Exchequer Towne Club.

4

The Chancellors of the Exchequer Arrive

The Exchequer is actually Noah's pride and joy. It was his first major business success. Noah didn't invent this nightclub concept, but he did it as well or better than his counterparts throughout the country.

"When I was a young man, I traveled a lot. I enjoyed hanging out at clubs like every other young person with money in our pockets and a hankering to see the world."

In Atlanta, the spot was Mr. V's and in Washington, DC, it was the Foxtrappe. In East St. Louis, he would go to the Blue Note. All over the country, in any city that had an iconic club for Black people, Noah checked it out and the experience had a strong effect on him. It was almost like he was doing market research, but didn't know to give his process that name.

"I always noticed the difference between those clubs and the nightclubs that catered to Black crowds in New Orleans. The New Orleans clubs were smaller, with no interior design, and felt more like a corner bar."

There was another person involved in the decision to bring big-city nightlife to New Orleans.

"My good friend, Sidney Richmond, was working as a med tech at Charity Hospital and I was a medical salesman for Mead Johnson Laboratories when we decided to do something different, something that could make a lot of money. We kicked around ideas of what it could be; it had to be something that lots of people would be willing to spend lots of money for. I suggested a jazz club or nightclub."

The two friends kept talking.

Noah brought up his experiences in the nightclub business, and they both agreed this idea could work. After a few days of brainstorming, they committed to the club proposition, but they faced a big stumbling block. Neither of them had any money.

"We wrote these fundamentals on a sheet of paper: seed money to get started, a working name for the club, a proposal to approach investors, a bank account, and a possible location."

Undaunted by their lack of capital, they put their thinking caps on. As they talked about the financial challenge, they came up with a concept. They would produce a minority business directory and use advertising sales to generate revenue. These funds would cover the cost of printing, and any amount left over would be their seed money for the club project. Then they kicked around possible names and decided on The Exchequer Towne Club.

"We didn't call ourselves owners, proprietors, or managing partners. We were the Chancellors of The Exchequer. We borrowed this from a country where the chancellor is in charge of the treasury. Remember, our goal was to make a lot of money."

Noah put his creative talents to work as the plan started taking shape. "Since I am a graphic designer, it was on me to design a logo."

Jointly, Noah and Sidney developed a proposal, and they each put up $100 to open a bank account. Then they worked on the *New Orleans Minority Business Directory*, formatted similar to the *Yellow Pages*, except it had green pages, symbolizing money. Directory listings ranged from accountants to upholsterers, with advertisers galore throughout the pages.

"We finished the directory with a surplus left in the bank account, then started our search for a club location."

Without the benefit of start-up advisors or business mentors, they still made all the right moves: a solid idea,

The Exchequer
Towne Club

6200 ELYSIAN FIELDS AVE.
NEW ORLEANS, LA. 70122
(504) 282-3210

SIDNEY RICHMOND, JR.
Chancellor of The Exchequer

business plan, conceptual prototype, market analysis, and early stage financing to do small things that improved their chances of attracting big bucks. With The Exchequer logo imprinted on high-quality golf shirts, business cards, letterhead, and professional brochures printed, they had put their seed money to good use. Ultimately, Noah and Sidney accomplished what they had set out to do. They gave New Orleans a nightclub

experience that rivaled iconic clubs in big cities. The location was 6200 Elysian Fields.

"I had passed that building thousands of times on my way to the lakefront and never paid that much attention to it. The building was seven thousand square feet and two stories, perfect for the mall concept we had in mind, giving our customers multiple options under one roof."

The Exchequer laid the foundation for NEXUS.

These twin success stories, The Exchequer followed by NEXUS, had taken root in his soul a long time ago. The dream started a little fuzzy; after all, Noah was from a poor family that lived in low-income neighborhoods where crushed business dreams lingered on every tattered sign and shuttered storefront. Even as a child, he knew he would escape this environment. He instinctively developed a winning formula: quality service, administrative efficiency, employee fulfillment, and customer satisfaction.

5

Natural Born Businessman

Thinking of his first business, he appreciated the value of a good street hustle. He was smart about making money and began building his bankroll when he was just seven years old. He had a business concept, keen marketing skills, and a couple of children who increased his capacity to deliver services on time at a reasonable price. Not bad for a child who had just learned to tie his shoes.

Over time, and after many experiences, he would grow into a respected business leader of national prominence.

Noah in military uniform.

After being discharged from the Army at the age of twenty, he worked as a consultant to a nightclub in St. Louis. Returning to New Orleans, he worked at a series of jobs, but he could not shake the entrepreneurship bug that bit him when he was a child. He had an insatiable need to create and manage his own business. He also aspired to provide jobs to people whose backgrounds may have been similar to his.

Just like he intuitively knew how to cultivate customers, Noah had all the other traits of a successful businessman: a will to win, an engaging personality, excellent communication skills, resourceful ways of overcoming obstacles, creativity, commitment, and confidence.

When he and Sidney teamed up, their partnership was a powerful energy that fueled their business momentum.

In 1980, Sidney died. He was a young man in the prime of his life. He had been Noah's best friend and business partner. Sidney was gone and Noah was shattered.

Noah with Sidney

In the aftermath, Noah's life turned upside down, but he persevered, put The Exchequer behind him, and invested his time, energy, and skills in a new club that gave him a fresh start.

33

In 1981, he found a quaint building on Esplanade Avenue with a cozy interior and walls that were perfect for acoustics. This was the location for Noah's, a jazz club that was small, warm, and ideal for jazz purists.

"The building was over two hundred years old and was located in a historic area on the edge of the French Quarter," Noah said, describing the location. "The brick floors and brick walls gave it a feeling of an old-time jazz club in the 1930s."

A 1982 gem in the newspaper talked about an enchanting evening at Noah's: *It was one of those you-had-to-be-there events 'cause there's no way to describe what went down and the music that went 'round. Regular performers at Noah's, pianist/vocalist Linda Aubert and vocalist Phillip Manuel (he's as pretty as he sings and is managed by legal eagle Bobby Richardson, nephew of barrister Lolis Elie), graciously relinquished one of their sets to sorceress Lady B.J. After she performed a piece of celestial hocus pocus, vocalist Laverne Butler did a turn at the mike.*

Published in *The Times-Picayune*, Betty Guillaud, indisputable queen of New Orleans society news had written these glowing words. Noah thanked the gods of good luck for smiling on him. White people with old money or good jobs religiously read Betty Gilllaud's column, and having this crowd see his club celebrated in that space was priceless publicity. Fortunately, his white clientele mixed comfortably with his Black customers. That's because jazz is a great equalizer. Opened for just a short time, Noah's Jazz Club had a good run.

In 1983, he returned to the same street corner where The Exchequer had been and opened NEXUS. Once again tapping into his business network, he landed new investors. Money for NEXUS came from Richard Powell, who was a pharmacy major at Xavier University and a classmate of Noah's first wife, Emma McAboy. Richard and Noah had played flag football on the Xavier campus and had developed a close friendship. Richard moved to Chicago after graduating from Xavier. He provided the initial seed money for NEXUS and recruited other investors, including businessmen in Chicago and Atlanta.

6

Ushering in the NEXUS Era

"I knew this as clear as night follows day; what people see can affect their mood. I wanted everybody to feel good when they first entered NEXUS and every other moment they spent there. That's why I designed the club with warm colors. I had brass accents sparkling like jewelry on a beautiful woman. And the lighting under the counter gave the club a soft glow."

Noah created a tantalizing experience that tingled every sensory perception. It was about the scene and being seen. And the music, from the dance beats upstairs to the live jazz downstairs, hit the right note. But being ready for guests on the night of the pre-opening was a struggle.

At one point on that Thursday night, Noah felt certain the club would not be ready for the pre-opening celebration and he spoke his fear out loud.

"The club was a mess when I said that; the piano tuner was late, carpet was still being laid in the downstairs bar, guys over there were assembling chairs, guys over here were hanging the brass wine glass holders, and everywhere I looked, something was unfinished.

"But my guys said, 'Oh no, we are going to do this.'

"We had hired a company from a suburb of New Orleans to do the drop ceilings, and the installer started packing up to leave at 4:45. That triggered a conversation between that man and my guys, who were not about to let that man walk out with the job undone.

"'Where are you going?'

"'I get off at 5:00.'

"'Oh no, you can't leave until this ceiling is finished.'

"'I have to call my boss.'

"'You better call him and get his okay to keep working.'

"When the man called, his boss refused to authorize overtime pay, so I asked what the rate was and told his boss I would cover the cost."

The man finished at 7:30 that evening.

"At that time, we had cars and people lined up outside. Upstairs was ready, so we let people in the side door and directed them to the dance club on the second floor. I think we had either LeBron Joseph or A.D. Berry deejaying and nobody knew what was happening downstairs." That was an experience Noah will never forget.

"We had worked thirty-six hours straight, but at 7:00 p.m., we all ran home, showered, and changed clothes. We came back and tried to enjoy opening night more tired than we had ever been.

"At nine o'clock, we made an announcement to the crowd upstairs that downstairs was open. The piano was tuned, the band was playing, bartenders were standing by their stations ready to take drink orders and servers were at the door greeting customers."

Noah continued reflecting on that big night. "People didn't see the tools and things we had stashed out of sight—all they noticed was the club, ready to rock and roll. The champagne fountains were flowing, and the food was set up. From that day on, NEXUS thrived."

And when Noah talks about NEXUS, he always compliments the house band.

"They were outta sight. Everybody loved the NEXUS musicians, and I was probably their biggest fan. They gave themselves the name Noah's Ark-kestra."

David Torkanowsky, Chris Severin, and Julian Garcia were jazz musicians whose live performances were reminiscent of Minton's Playhouse. A mural depicting Duke Ellington surrounded by sophisticated ladies overlooked a white, baby grand piano; a tribute to the music that was the lifeblood of the Cotton Club.

Upstairs at NEXUS was for high-energy dancing and was probably where Percy "Master P" Miller, founder of No Limits Records, partied when he was a young man.

This was long before Master P's earnings reached $200 million, a net worth derived from music, movies, investments, and business. This rags to riches story with New Orleans roots captivated a prime-time TV audience in July 2020. The program motivated Kristian Newman to call me, excited about that revelation from Master P, which he shared with the world. We were tickled to hear that Master P met the woman who would become his wife at NEXUS. And they were probably upstairs, where the deejay kept the dance floor packed all night.

Downstairs, the bar was eye candy. It was also a magnet that drew customers like bees to honey.

Positioned in the center of the club, Noah had a strategy about liquor placement. On prominent display were Chivas Regal, Remy Martin, and other premium brands in the front row; irresistible temptations to customers with excellent taste, those who were grandiose show-offs, and people who were bourgeoisie impostors.

Top shelf brands were behind the expensive labels. Well-drinks were tucked away, but available for anyone who was balling on a budget.

NEXUS catered to a predominantly Black crowd of professionals who flexed their economic muscle with the fancy cars they drove, expensive clothes they wore, and affluent neighborhoods where they lived. Noah gave them and the "want-to-be-like-them" a place to mix and mingle.

Just as Noah and I met at NEXUS, hundreds of other couples also made a love connection there, including Adele Tennyson and George Williams. "We dated, got married, and had our son, Jordan."

She recalled what NEXUS meant to Black people in New Orleans.

"It was the Who's Who for us. When Black entertainers came to the city and asked where to go, everybody told them NEXUS."

Adele was often there when celebrities came through.

"I met Phyllis Hyman there, Benson, the TV actor was in there, Patti LaBelle, Stevie Wonder, Sister Sledge." She added, "I thoroughly enjoyed that aspect, but I also enjoyed the camaraderie, and you couldn't find a better happy hour. To me, there was nothing better to do on a weekend. There was NEXUS and before NEXUS, there was The Exchequer."

7

When We Became a Couple

I felt at ease here.

I had been in New Orleans for two months when I first visited NEXUS. Greeted warmly by staff and customers, I was surprised and appreciative that so many people knew my name. After all, these were viewers and in TV news, you live and die by the size of your audience. One after the other, men bought me drinks as an entrée to flirtation. However, my new friend Jezelle, who obviously frequented NEXUS, had a plan that involved just one man. She found the club's owner and brought him over to meet me.

"So, you moved here from Houston?" Noah asked.

With a smile in my voice, I said, "Do you know much about Houston?"

He said, "I have a lot of friends there, like Kenny Burrough, Robert Brazile, and some other football players with the Houston Oilers."

"Well, you must know Adrian and Cookie," I responded, referring to Kenny's girlfriend and Robert's wife.

Our lighthearted banter continued until he excused himself to get back to work, but not before he made sure we could reconnect some other time.

"I know you are new in town, so here's my card. I'm writing my home number on the back. Call me anytime."

That was on a Friday night. I called him that Saturday afternoon. Wanting nothing more than a platonic relationship, that's exactly how things started. We became good friends who enjoyed each other's company. Since we talked about everything, I knew he was a big-time player.

The first question I would ask any time I went to NEXUS was, "Is this a 20% night, or is it 80%?" The question was my way of determining whether he had slept with a low or high number of the female customers who were in the building.

But it really didn't matter because a romantic relationship was not even possible for us. When it came to dating, we were different species; he was from Mars and I was from Venus.

"I have major trust issues," I confessed to Noah one day when he came to visit me.

The club was still popping both upstairs and downstairs when he left. He had assigned a manager to close out the registers, count the money, bag it for bank deposit, and lock it in the club's safe.

Free to leisurely drive from the club to my place, Noah actually enjoyed the stars twinkling in the pre-dawn sky.

He knew my schedule and didn't mind coming to my apartment for coffee and conversation, as I got dressed for work. Full of jokes, he always made me laugh. Here's one I remember.

"There was this ninety-year-old man who married a twenty-five-year-old woman. When his friends asked him if he was afraid of dying, the old guy said, 'Not concerned, not one bit. If she dies, she dies.'"

But this day was different. This man was different. I felt comfortable sharing a part of my story that I kept tucked deep inside.

To give me some extra time and a boost of courage, I asked him about the worst thing that happened to him as a child.

"My mother used to get hand-me-down clothes from white people," Noah said, reflecting on how this became the source of a major childhood embarrassment. "One day after all my brothers and sisters got through picking out their school clothes for that day, all that was left for me were these purple pants with a pink satin stripe on each leg. I wore them, but I felt like a circus clown."

"How old were you?

"I was probably nine or ten, in the fourth or fifth grade at Paul Lawrence Dunbar Elementary in Gert Town."

This opened the door for me to talk about my childhood.

Mentally traveling back in time, I pictured myself in my little pleated skirt that was a plaid pattern of pink and gray, fashionably coordinated with a gray cashmere sweater, pink socks, and pink ribbons on my three braids.

"My first day of school, I was just four years old," I said, sharing a fond memory. "My mom held my hand as we walked from our house down the street to Doty Elementary. She has been my safety net my whole life."

"What about your father?"

"Never met him," I responded, explaining how they became my parents. "He was a neighbor boy, living in the Sojourner projects. That's where my mother lived, too, when she was growing up. His name was Phillip Stapleton, and he walked my mom home from school one day. They were in the house alone. Mother Nature took over and five months later, my mother realized she was pregnant. He never acknowledged me and went on with his life. After high school, he joined the Navy, married another woman, and they started a family."

Continuing, I said, "At school, they used to give us these cards at the beginning of the school year. I hated checking the box next to 'Illegitimate.' It made me feel ashamed and filthy. So, I created my own coping strategy."

Confessing how insecure I had been as a child, I told him I used academic excellence to get acceptance.

"I had learned to read when I was three years old. Funny how that happened," I told Noah, as I described my life at that young age.

We lived with my grandparents, Thomas Grant, and his second wife, Edna, who we called "Mimmie." Her son, Junior, had two boys, Terry and Tony. Along with my mother's two sisters, Willa Etta and Beatrice, we all shared the same three-bedroom, one-bathroom house on Calvert Street in a racially transitioning neighborhood in Detroit.

While the babysitter, "Auntie LaLa" to me, was teaching my cousin, Tony, to read, I was in the room, too, as an infant then toddler, learning by osmosis. I was three years old when my family first realized I could read and comprehend written material.

"I was way ahead of my classmates when I started kindergarten. My teacher decided that I was so advanced, she skipped me ahead to the first grade."

Glancing at the clock, I realized it was time for me to hit the highway. "Noah, let's finish this conversation later."

I ended the storytelling and headed for the front door while Noah undressed, knowing he was welcome to curl up in my bed and sleep while I was at work.

8

Our Dating Days

After receiving that day's marching orders from the assignment editor, Lloyd Edwards and I expected a productive day. We had become staunch partners, like Marvin and Tammi or Batman and Robin.

After a few hours in the field, gathering B-roll, conducting interviews, and shooting my standups, I returned to the TV station to complete two packaged news reports and two anchor voice-overs into sound bites. My workday over, I met Noah for lunch at Flagons on Magazine Street.

These were carefree days for us, getting to know each other, just two friends gliding through life, with no strings and no pressure.

We had spent every day together since the first night we met. Each time we talked, we shared a different chapter of our lives.

Noah had attended Priestly Junior High School in Pigeon Town and yearned to participate in school plays, yet he never could do this.

"My parents could not afford the costumes, so I had to settle for painting the props. I had to accept that even though I wasn't on stage, at least my work was."

Noah's family, with eleven siblings, was large and loving. His mother, Florence, was the glue that held everyone together—her children and her grandchildren.

With his mother as the mortar, his father was the brick and together they built a home inside a house united.

Noah said, "My father would work even when he was sick. I remember many times that he held two jobs at the same time. And he took care of all of us, treated all the kids the same, even my sisters and brothers who were not his biological children."

While we were still in our friendship phase, Noah told his mother and his business partner he was going to marry me. I had no idea this was his plan and would have shot it down since I had a clearly defined plan that did not include marriage.

Essentially wedded to my career, I preferred an uncomplicated personal life. Noah was a one-man soap opera who could have inspired scripts for *All My Children*. But as a friend, he was a blessing, and he had a lot of great qualities. I especially admired his work ethic.

"I started my first business when I was seven years old...shoeshine service, pickup and delivery and I even had employees...two other boys in the Gert Town neighborhood who were the same age as me."

Born to be an entrepreneur, Noah put his business dreams on hold when days after graduating from high school, he joined the Army.

"The Army was my way of getting military benefits so I could go to college."

I really admired this man with a plan.

As we left my apartment headed to lunch, we drove from St. Charles Avenue toward downtown, around Lee Circle.

"Do you know the history of that statue?' Noah asked, as I strained to see the confederate monument standing on a tall base that stretched high into the sky.

"That statue honors General Robert E. Lee, which is why this area is called Lee Circle. I think it was called Tivoli Circle before that."

Rounding the curve, we were now parallel to the streetcar line. I giggled, prompting Noah to ask, "What's so funny?"

"That little boy just stuck his tongue out at me and put his hands behind his ears, looking like Dumbo the elephant."

We crossed several streets — Julia, Girod, Lafayette, Poydras and kept driving until we reached Canal Street (packed with tourists), turned left, drove a short distance to Basin Street (anchored by Krauss department store), turned right, and kept driving. As Basin became Orleans Avenue, Noah shared a bit of Mardi Gras culture with me.

"This is where all the Mardi Gras Indians meet up after the parades on Mardi Gras day."

"Excuse me, but who and what are Mardi Gras Indians?"

Noah, even though he could not prove it, had always been told that during slavery, indigenous Indians helped slaves escape. This built up a respect for Indians that Black men never lost. So, when they started their own Mardi Gras traditions, Black men in New Orleans showed gratitude to the Indians by respectfully imitating that culture.

"Each neighborhood has a tribe, and their costumes are called suits with unbelievable designs…made with beads, sequins, and feathers; seeing which tribe and chief have the best suits is my favorite part of Mardi Gras."

Mardi Gras indian.

Noah continued this fascinating history lesson, still driving to a destination unknown to me. Captivated by his knowledge, I listened as he talked about the old days of Mardi Gras when Black people were excluded from participating.

"So, we created our own ways of crashing the party. We put our own spin on it, not trying to be like the stuffy old-line Mardi Gras crowd from uptown. We added flavor and soul to Mardi Gras with the Baby Dolls and the Zulus and, of course, the Indians."

Continuing our drive, the conversation switched gears as Noah said, "We are now passing the Lafitte projects."

"Were these projects named after the pirate Jean Lafitte?"

"Don't know."

Noah steered the Cadillac Seville into a parking spot on the side of a small house on Orleans Avenue.

The white façade and black shutters were classic for homes in the New Orleans 6th ward. We got out of the car and walked up a few stairs, flanked by iron guardrails. Noah opened the door and I swear, I heard angels singing.

"This artwork is stunning," I said, mesmerized by museum-quality masterpieces.

Passing by an Elizabeth Catlett original surrounded by other superb works of art, we were seated at a table directly across from a painting by Jacob Lawrence in the company of Romare Bearden, John Scott, and William Tolliver creations.

While my eyes were ingesting the visual feast, tantalizing aromas were setting off alarms inside my body like a fire truck rushing to a burning building.

And just reading the menu made my mouth water—andouille, boudin, dirty rice, veal parmesan, gumbo, etouffee, jambalaya, bread pudding, and other tasty New Orleans dishes. The chef, Leah Chase, was a national treasure with a down-home personality that made everyone feel special.

As I ate my stuffed mirliton and Noah enjoyed a shrimp po' boy sandwich, he talked.

"If the walls of this restaurant could talk..." he said, his voice trailing off.

Noah loved his hometown and was always willing to talk about the fascinating people, places, and projects that had carved their imprint on her tale.

Dooky Chase had been around since 1939. It was originally a small sandwich shop founded by Edgar "Dooky" Chase, Sr., with ownership later transferred to Dooky Jr. and his wife, Leah. In the 1950s, when it was illegal for Blacks and whites to be in each other's company, Dooky and Leah Chase defied the law. They were at the forefront of the Civil Rights Movement and welcomed mixed-race customers into their dining room for meetings. But it wasn't always about Civil Rights. They were on the side of people's rights.

"You should make a point to meet people who have been fighting the good fight a long time. Look to your left. There's Tom Dent sitting with lawyer Lolis Elie."

During this conversation he elaborated on many unapologetic champions of Black empowerment: A.P. Tureaud, Avery Alexander, Judge Israel Augustine, Jerome

Smith, and Rudy Lombard. I found it curious that only one woman's name was mentioned—Oretha Castle Haley. Noah had just opened my eyes to astonishing facts and legendary figures.

"These people are living history and the meetings they held here at Dooky Chase were epic."

Pausing from the storytelling, Noah chewed his food and took a big swallow of iced tea.

I knew Noah was popular with women. I now saw his popularity through a different lens.

A classic Creole beauty with caramel skin, smooth as butter, seemed to be moving in our direction. Her silky straight hair that once hung below her waist was cut in a short style befitting an elegant woman with a busy job.

All heads turned as she walked into the room where diners were eating. Flashing her one-thousand-watt smile that was notorious for melting the hearts of powerful men, her eyes were set on the man seated across from me.

"Hey, Mr. Noah, so glad to see you," Leah Chase said, pushing back an extra chair at our table. The moment she sat down she instantly displayed her charm.

"You know I work from sunup to sundown, but don't be surprised if you spot me on a bar stool one night. I'm hearing great things about what you're doing."

She pointed to a waitress named Patrice servicing a nearby table, and another waiter named Tommy taking an order from customers. She said they worked for her in the daytime, worked at NEXUS in the evenings, and often commented that Noah was a wonderful boss. Changing the subject, she became the quintessential host.

"How's your food? And who is this pretty lady you brought with you?"

"Let me introduce you. Leah Chase meet Karin Grant. You'll be seeing a lot of her. She's on the news on Channel 8 and she is also my special friend."

I immediately liked Leah Chase and loved her restaurant. As a journalist, I saw possible story angles everywhere I looked. I made a mental note to check the newsroom archives to see what stories we had covered involving this restaurant and pitch anything we had missed. I really wanted to do a story on the fabulous art collection.

"Nice to meet you and you are welcome here any time, with him or without him," Leah Chase said as she pushed her chair back and rose.

Slightly leaning over Noah's back, she graciously let us know she was moving on to other business.

"Mr. Noah, thanks for coming by and Karin, I see you tried the mirlitons today. Next time, call me before you come. I'm going to fix something that I only serve to my favorite customers."

"Noah, if I catch this woman in here by herself, you better watch out," a man said as Leah walked back to the restaurant's kitchen.

"Man, how you doing?" Noah said, standing up to shake hands.

"Have you met Karin Grant?"

"Haven't met her, but I am in love with her and have intimate relations with her every day in my bedroom."

Awkward silence.

"What I'm saying is, I watch her on TV every morning as I am laying in my bed. I must say, you are even more beautiful in person."

"Karin…this man used to be my friend. But as of this conversation, he is no longer on my Christmas card list."

We laughed. The man (who shall remain unnamed) left and we continued eating lunch. It didn't take long for Noah to resume talking again. This time it was about his days in the military. He and his friends frequented several bars in St. Louis about one hundred miles from their Army base in Waynesville, Missouri.

"Yeah, there were a couple of clubs we used to hit on weekends, but there was something about this one bar that I liked… Can't remember the name of it, but the owner, I think his name was Willie. He was a musician and I used to talk to him all the time when I went in there."

They would engage in small talk, "chit chat" was Noah's description.

"How's the crowd? How's business going tonight?"

Frustrated, the owner would share his financial problems. "I'm just not making any money. I have a crowd of people in here, but the money side of things is bad."

Noah felt he knew why the business was failing. The club was arranged all wrong. The dance floor was situated at the entrance. This created a barricade for people trying to get to the bar. As the crowd was swaying and swinging to Mary Wells, Wilson Pickett, The Supremes, Temptations, Impressions, and other chart-topping R&B recording artists, these packed bodies were problem #1. But Noah also had identified other issues.

"The place was dark as a dungeon, with red lights. Plus, the booze on the shelf was just sporadic…nothing felt right."

Finally, one evening, Noah offered to help. He suggested a few simple changes that would instantly boost revenues.

"You don't have a cover charge. That's money that could add to your bottom line. And the way this place is set up, with all these people dancing as soon as they come in because they hear the music the deejay is playing, makes no sense. Your customers are not buying drinks. They never get to the bar and the bar is where you should be making your money."

Our conversation flowed as easily as the sweet tea from the pitcher the waiter held as he refilled Noah's glass.

"How old were you when you took on this challenge?"

"I was twenty, one-month shy of turning twenty-one."

"What experience did you have managing nightclubs?"

"None. I had a gut feeling, and that was it. At the time I was talking to him, I didn't have the foggiest idea about how I was going to get it done. I just knew some things needed to be done."

"So, you were basically working off raw instincts?"

"I saw that this bar and all the others around town looked the same way…red carpet, red lights, too much red. I figured if the club was more inviting and had better logistics, it would be better for his net income. I told the guy it's going to mean a little sacrifice when you close down for about two weeks to make changes, but the sacrifice will pay off."

Of course, the owner wanted to know what these changes would cost. Noah offered a best guess. "Probably between three and five thousand dollars, but it's an investment in your business."

The owner agreed and hired Noah, who had no track record, just a head full of ideas and the confidence of a young man just entering adulthood, ready to make bold moves.

"I reconfigured the place and corrected that dance floor mess. I wanted to entice customers to buy drinks more than anything else since that's where the revenue comes from. I switched things around to make the bar the focal point."

Noah wanted customers to drink first, dance later, and then keep drinking all night long. Taking the booze from out of the back in the storage room, he put all the liquor on display, and added flashing lights and a mirror ball over the dance floor, now positioned for better flow and more liquor sales. He retrained all the waiters and bartenders to make them a part of the new and improved customer experience.

After being closed for two weeks to implement the changes, the club reopened with spectacular flair. It was a two-step process that became a signature Noah Hopkins strategy for club openings. He designed invitations announcing a special VIP pre-opening and mailed them to regular customers and important people in St. Louis. Noah scheduled this preview event on a Sunday for a strategic reason.

"I wanted to get people talking about the new look and feel of the club when they went to work on Monday. This was my way of stoking word-of-mouth publicity for the actual reopening later that week."

The following Thursday, when the club officially had its second coming, was an exciting experience. Noah recalled the scene in vivid detail.

"It was like a Hollywood movie premier. There was food, champagne, and music, all free. We had a neon sign on the building, tracking lights beaming bright streams into the sky, limousines parked outside, and all employees dressed in crisp black pants and shirts. In other words, I changed the atmosphere and made an impression…and just like I planned…this place was the talk of the town."

The club became popular and profitable.

Noah learned a lot from that experience, mostly about himself. He was creative yet cost-conscious, had a keen business sense, a knack for customer engagement, and killer marketing skills, and he also had developed a formula for future nightclubs he would later own, operate, and drive to phenomenal success.

After leaving Missouri, he came back home. When he left New Orleans, he was a teenage boy. When he returned, he was a young man with GI benefits. He lived with his older sister, Fern, worked wherever he could find a job, and attended Southern University of New Orleans.

In his early twenties, he bought a sports car and was in a Corvette club. He started a T-shirt business, sold insurance, managed a bar called Caesar's East, was a pharmaceutical sales rep, and an emerging businessman.

We learned so much about each other over shared meals, sometimes at dine-in restaurants and other times with pickup orders.

Our list included Que Sera, Chez Helene, Fitzgerald's, Dunbar's, Barrow's, Stephen & Martin's, Uglesich's, Camellia Grill, Commander's Palace, Ralph & Kacoo's, Feelings; the list goes on and on.

On weekends we always ended our nights at NEXUS, but often would start the evening visiting friendly competitors, like the Bottom Line, Brass Bull, and Touch of Class. We also occasionally went to 4141 and Georgie Porgie's.

We rode the streetcar, walked the Riverfront, sauntered through the French Market, and relaxed at the lake.

One night, we stayed in, lounging at Noah's townhouse in New Orleans East. We sipped wine and listened to his collection of jazz albums on a vintage stereo record player. I felt safe, safe enough to share my deepest, darkest secret with my best friend.

"When I was eight, my mother bought a house on the west side of Detroit. She was only twenty-four years old, working at Kanners and Patrize, a small wholesale shoe supply store on Second Avenue. I was a smart student, doing well in my classes at St. Theresa Catholic School. My mother was really strict, and I was not allowed to let anyone in the house or go outside when she was at work."

As I continued talking about this time in my life, Noah quietly listened.

I talked about getting good grades and being a smart, obedient little girl. I recalled rebelling a little when I was twelve years old and giving a cute boy in the neighborhood my phone number. After a few phone calls, one day he asked me to meet him at the confectionary store on Beechwood.

"He bought me a bottle of Faygo's orange pop. We walked around the corner to an apartment that was obviously familiar to him. Inside, there was an older man. His name was Jessie. It was clear I had been lured into a sex trap that ended badly for me. After putting my clothes back on, I walked home by myself. I took a long, hot bath and curled up in my bed… Never told anybody that I had been raped."

That night, Noah became more than my friend. He exorcised demons that had consumed me since I was a twelve-year-old adolescent. I felt liberated, like I had been in an informal therapy session and lost two tons of shame.

As I typed that memory on my computer, Luther Vandross was singing these lyrics, "*It surely was the best thing I ever did… The night when I fell in love… The stars' lights were in your eyes… The night that I fell in love… with you*" In my loudest voice, I shouted, "*Yes*" remembering that was the night. That was the night I fell in love with Noah Hopkins, a certified playboy and unabashed Casanova.

Karin and Noah, New Year's Eve 1986

Not only was he taken, but he was also entangled in a web of women. Certain that he had feelings for me, too, I did what I do best; I came up with a strategic plan. I told Noah I would accept his relationship with his girlfriend of two years. To protect her privacy, I will not use her name. I confess I was being intentionally conniving when I told Noah that he could date both of us.

This was a big, fat lie. I had no intention of sharing him. My game plan was simple and relied on my strengths counterbalanced against her weaknesses. I knew that between the two of us, I would be more attractive because I was calm, stable, and willing to give him space. She, on the other hand, was bound to become hysterical and demanding as she watched her hold on him slipping away. Noah and I were equals, and we were building a strong partnership. Comparing the two, the scales tipped considerably in my favor.

Our romance was on a fast track. He had a key to my apartment, and I had a key to his townhouse. We would alternate where we stayed—one week at my place, the next week at his. Packing up one evening, I handed something to him to pack in my bag. Instead, he stuck it in his pocket.

We stopped at Delchamps, a grocery store on the I-10 service road in New Orleans East. Waiting in the checkout line, a woman standing behind him said, "You 'bout to lose your bra."

Noah, usually quick with a comeback, was at a loss for words. Such was the life of transient lovers in the fast lane.

But my bra dangling from his pocket in a public place was a small incident compared to what was ahead.

My prediction about the wrath of a scorned woman came true.

9

One Woman Too Many

The first time it happened was during the 1986 National Association of Television Program Executives (NATPE) convention. Held in New Orleans a few times, this event moves around the world. It always attracts enormous crowds, including high-ranking television executives with godlike power concerning what we watch on TV. Lucky producers get picked up by a network or syndicator, and their programs could become the next big hit. Television's hottest stars also come to NATPE to connect with industry big shots. Noah and I attended the convention back when King World Productions syndicated the *Oprah Winfrey Show* and the queen of talk was the biggest celebrity there.

In the evenings after the convention shut down, there were private parties held all over the city. Essence magazine had big goals concerning television and had launched a talk show called *Essence Style* anchored by the iconic Susan Taylor.

Essence hosted a private reception at WDSU TV, a New Orleans television station affiliated with NBC. Clarence Smith, a good friend of Noah's and one of the men who founded Essence magazine, invited Noah and I was his date. A photographer from *The Times-Picayune* took a picture of us laughing with *Essence* executive, Gene Davis, and Karen Thomas, director of sales promotion and merchandising at Essence. This picture appeared in the next day's newspaper.

Seeing the picture sent his other girlfriend into a rage that started with a series of screaming phone calls and continued when she caught up with Noah at NEXUS. He escorted her into his office in the back of the club as she continually threatened to go into the public space and make a scene. With a large group from the NATPE convention at NEXUS that night, this would have been a much worse embarrassment than the purple and pink pants incident from his childhood.

Actress Marla Gibbs was there with an entourage from Hollywood. Beloved as the wise-cracking maid on *The Jeffersons* TV show, she adored New Orleans and NEXUS was her favorite nightspot. Noah had sent word to me through a manager about the fire he was trying to extinguish, so I became his surrogate host.

After the club closed, I drove my car to his townhouse, and he said, "Thanks for holding things down tonight. She just would not listen to reason. I finally talked her into leaving with me so we could spend some private time together. We left out the back door, went someplace for a cup of coffee, and

I took her home. It's a miracle that I was able to do all that, rush back before we closed and still spend a little time with Marla Gibbs before she left the club."

10

Our Wedding Adventure

After eighteen months of dating, Noah talked about making our relationship permanent. He didn't get down on one knee and pop open a ring box. It was more like a comfortable conversation.

Noah had one major stumbling block; he was still married to his second wife, Shirley Harmon Hopkins. When I met Noah, they had been separated for quite a while but had never bothered to get a divorce. Now that he needed to tie up that loose end, he told Shirley he planned to make it official and end their marriage. That was a very uncomfortable conversation.

Thinking a wedding had to be an elaborate production, I started doing the things required of a bride-to-be: planning a guest list, selecting a venue, making a checklist, wedding gown, caterer, cake design, invitations, and then one day this process came to a screeching halt. Neither of us wanted this type of wedding.

"Let's go to Vegas and get married and at a tacky little chapel and maybe even have an Elvis impersonator…"

We got excited about this plan and decided July 4, 1987, would be our wedding day. The same artist who painted the *Sophisticated Ladies* mural at NEXUS, Harry Wilson, designed our wedding announcement card.

We invited our good friends, Harry and Brenda Williams, to join us in Las Vegas. We could not get a hotel reservation, so we booked rooms in Los Angeles and rented a car for the four-hour drive.

We were all set until Noah called Shirley to see if she had signed the divorce papers. This was three months before the wedding, and she was not cooperating.

In May 1987, Noah had a business meeting in Miami and I tagged along. This was where he bought my engagement ring. After we returned, we quietly resumed our lives, which for me meant delivering the news to a television audience. His former girlfriend noticed the bling on my left hand and called to bless him, but not in a nice way.

That became a campaign of harassment with her and her friends doing things that junior high school girls do to annoy somone on their hit list.

Besides this ex-girlfriend's silliness, there was the estranged wife. Conversations about the divorce triggered arguments and our wedding plans appeared hopeless.

But a miracle happened. Noah got a phone call from Shirley. She said she had signed the divorce papers and was overnighting them to him by special delivery mail. This was two days before we were to leave for our wedding trip.

On July 3, we flew into Los Angeles, rented a car, and checked into a hotel.

The next day, Noah and I hopped in the front seats of our rented Cadillac while Harry and Brenda slid into the back seats and we headed to Las Vegas. When we hit Death Valley, we saw road signs that read: Avoid Overheating, Turn off AC next 20 Miles. "It's too hot to drive for twenty miles with no air conditioning," Noah said, as we all basically echoed, "Amen" in agreement.

A California state trooper stopped us for speeding. Noah flipped open his wallet, deliberately flashing his Orleans Parish Reserve Deputy badge. Taking notice, the officer extended professional courtesy and let us go with a warning. But his attention quickly turned away from us and onto a car that had pulled directly in front of us. The driver got out and started peeing on the shoulder of the highway. That guy got a ticket, maybe for indecent exposure. He should have gotten a second citation for stupidity.

When we arrived in Las Vegas that July 4, the temperature was well over one hundred degrees. We stopped at a casino to ask for directions to the place that issued wedding licenses. The air conditioning felt so good, it was hard to leave that building. But we eventually pulled ourselves out of this comfort zone and stepped back into the sweltering heat.

We drove to the courthouse, showed our IDs to the clerk, paid the fee, and received a document authorizing us to legally marry. A short distance away, we found the Little White Chapel.

Noah paid $200 for the "Love and Cherish" package. He perused the music catalog, selected "Suddenly" by Billy Ocean as our wedding song, picked a floral bouquet for me and a silk boutonniere for himself. Photography came with the package. Harry and Brenda were our witnesses as Noah and I said "I do" to seal our vows.

The reason we booked a hotel room in Los Angeles was that Las Vegas had been booked solid on July 4. After hitting every casino on the strip at 1:30 in the morning, I checked the front desk at the Golden Nugget Hotel to see if any rooms had become available. Jackpot! There had been two cancellations. I immediately booked those rooms. Exhausted, Brenda and I retired for the night while the guys continued to play at the blackjack table.

At six o'clock, the morning after our wedding, Noah came to our room, pleased with the winnings he had pocketed. He was starving for food and a little honeymoon indulgence. After breakfast, we checked out and headed back to Los Angeles where we spent our remaining time shopping in the garment district and since Noah was flush with cash, I was free to splurge.

We flew back home to New Orleans and settled into married life.

11

Three Decades and Counting

Noah and I have been married since 1987. Always the funny guy, we cracked up when Noah said he looks in the mirror now and asks his reflection, "Who the flock are you?"

Maybe it's time for Botox, hair color, and liposuction, but adult diapers and support socks? Not us, not yet anyway.

Fifteen years ago, we chose a new place to call home. We live six hours from New Orleans in driving distance but are worlds apart in terms of culture.

New Orleans is a small city with a big personality, and there was always something fascinating to see and do. After working all week, I rewarded myself on Saturdays with meandering strolls down Magazine Street, casually dipping in and out of antique shops and furniture stores.

The French Quarter bustled every day with tourists dropping their normal way of behaving to *laissez bon temp rouler* to the point of joining funeral processions and dancing to the rhythms of a brass band returning from a graveyard.

Few of these visitors knew they were taking part in a ritual with slave roots. Africans brought to New Orleans for slave labor celebrated the newfound freedom of a departed slave with music and dancing. Over time, the experience morphed into jazz funerals that have become one of the most renowned traditions in New Orleans, it's something that establishes this city as a unique treasure.

After the oil and gas industry abandoned New Orleans in the 1980s, tourism became the lifeblood of the New Orleans economy, but the overwhelming numbers of tourists could often be annoying.

Most leisure visitors would come to New Orleans to eat, drink, and sightsee. They clogged the streets and did not understand nor care about us; people who lived and worked in New Orleans. We had meetings and responsibilities that brought us into the Central Business District and the adjacent French Quarter. Wild people wandering through the streets without a care in the world would step in front of your car, causing you to move at a snail's pace. Noah and I would fantasize about a law that would give residents a quota of thirty tourists a day that we could legally run over with our cars. This was a cruel, insensitive joke, especially for Noah, whose customer base was sometimes half tourists.

New Orleans has stunning architecture, which reflects the cultural and ethnic mix that makes the city so endearing. For example, African slaves constructed the wrought-iron railings, narrow balconies, and wider galleries in the French Quarter under the direction of French and Spanish overseers.

This city is comprised of multiple neighborhoods, each with its own distinct identity and all worth exploring, though back in the 1980s, public housing developments, including the Desire, Calliope, St. Bernard, and St. Thomas, were notoriously dangerous.

Noah knew every nook and corner in New Orleans and was happy to live there until one day when he wasn't. In 2004, we moved to Alabama and settled into a quieter life with a slower pace.

Where we live now is a small town with an impressive history. We're in Tuskegee, with about eight thousand five hundred permanent residents. The population increases when Tuskegee University students are in school.

Our home is spacious and sits on a one-acre lot with mature magnolia trees providing a lovely fragrance and canopies of shade. The exterior has a wraparound porch and tall columns.

Inside, there is a beautiful rich cherry-stained staircase, original pocket doors, antique chandeliers, and hardwood floors laid by nineteenth-century artisans.

We often comment that God plucked us out of New Orleans in 2004 to show us mercy, knowing we had experienced our share of flood-related heartache throughout the years.

In May 1995, New Orleans had forty hours of rain. Unfortunately for us, our house on South Galvez Street sat on a flat foundation and was at the bottom of a slope in the city's layout. All that runoff drained toward us, and since we lived in the equivalent of a bowl, we were doomed. Disoriented by the sheer magnitude of what was happening, we stayed until we had four feet of water inside our home.

As the water continued to rise, we walked to our next-door neighbor's home, which was a two-story construction. Simply walking to the house next door took forever in such horrible conditions. It was pitch black outside, and we were trudging against heavy water, making every step feel like we had a ton of bricks tied to our feet. When we finally made it to higher ground, we exhaled.

As bad as that was, we had experienced something even worse.

In 1993, we were awakened about midnight by a noise. Water was rushing into the house from heavy rainfall, causing small tables to move and objects to fall. We looked over the side of our bed and saw water rushing into our bedroom. When Noah spoke these words, he became my real-life superhero.

"The TVs, radio, and lamps are still plugged into the wall sockets. I will probably get electrocuted when I put my feet on the floor. But with me taking the shock, it will spare you."

What do you say to someone willing to sacrifice his life for you?

At that moment, there were no words, just the actions of a husband who had accepted death so his wife could live. Noah inched to the edge of the bed and I cringed as he stood up.

My mind could see every electrical socket in the house, some located low, near baseboards, and I knew just like he had said, with the live voltage running through those circuits, feeding lamps, TVs, radios, our computer; the house was a giant death trap. This lethal combination of water and electricity was threatening to zap Noah like aluminum in a microwave. In the span of a few minutes, we experienced a roller coaster of emotions. Heart-stopping fear. Then mind-blowing relief. Grateful, we are still mystified that the electrical current we were expecting to surge through Noah's body did not happen.

We stayed in New Orleans after those nightmares, often talking about relocating to another city. In March 2004, we sold our house, closed our business, and moved away. Of course, this preceded Hurricane Katrina, which devastated New Orleans with massive flooding in 2005. What drove us to Alabama and how we became an asset to many lost, desperate Katrina survivors are stories for another book.

Sitting in the downstairs parlor, converted to a home office, I appreciate the art that decorates the walls. It softens the ache since I know what it means to miss New Orleans.

Masterpieces created by Richard Thomas, Terrence Osborne, Lionel Milton, George Rodrigue, and other New Orleans artists are a part of the sweet memories of a precious time in my life. Admittedly eclectic, my taste covers a wide range. We have an original Art Bacon portrait, Ronald McDowell abstracts, a Woodrow Nash sculpture, African masks, Cuban art, rare collector's editions of Jazzfest posters, bamboo rain sticks, lithographs, tribal tikis, and a hand-painted French silk batik. Noah, who is also an artist, has gifted me with two paintings he created that I cherish. When people comment on my art, I think back to the day I walked into Dookie Chase and marveled at the art collection on display there.

My office is serene and a great place to work on the independent projects I accept. I had set up this environment after I ended the corporate communications phase of my career and began working as a consultant.

So, I was ahead of the curve when the business world experienced a seismic shift, emptying office buildings and sending millions of workers to the safety of their homes to work remotely.

In December 2019, the country started hearing about a potential pandemic called the coronavirus. By March 2020, this health crisis, which was renamed COVID-19, shook this country with the force of a tectonic plate shift.

After being told to minimize contact with the outside world, my first act was to rush to Sam's in nearby Opelika to stock up on toilet paper.

I was shocked to find empty store shelves. I then rushed to Walmart in Auburn and bought multiple packages of paper products. I still don't know why my doomsday instinct turned me into a fool for toilet paper and paper towels. In my defense, I wasn't the only person irrationally reacting to COVID-19 in this way.

2020 was a year we will never forget. Throughout the country, working from home became the norm and almost everybody became an expert with Zoom technology for business meetings. This change made it easy for me to function as a consultant to Dr. Kyshun Webster, a brilliant businessman who is a true innovator. A child of New Orleans, this young man has consistently impressed me since I met him as a sixteen-year-old student at McMain High School. He is an unstoppable force. When he sets his mind to something, you better roll with him or get rolled over. He stepped into the business arena, with a focus on human enrichment and has been a trailblazing pioneer in his area of expertise.

Along with work commitments, I was also a caregiver to my elderly, sick, and widowed mother. Honestly, my hands were full. But I devoted my spare time to this book, and I am grateful for this project. After thirty-plus years of being together, I learned new things about Noah's past life.

12

The Consummate Businessman

Despite the girlfriend drama, business was Noah's true mistress. Business had been his first love since he developed a client base in his neighborhood, making seventy-five cents for each pair of shoes picked up and returned clean and shiny.

Back then, Noah demonstrated remarkable customer service. He also proved he was an excellent administrator by managing his staff and everything else related to his business with exceptional efficiency. By the way, he paid each employee ten cents. After the cost of supplies, he was happy with his profit margin. This level of business judgment was impressive for a seven-year-old child.

As a young teenager, he found another way to earn money.

"I was probably thirteen or fourteen when I worked for my uncle Dave at Foster's Road House, a small neighborhood bar in Hollygrove."

The bar, stocked from the counter to the ceiling with liquor, fascinated Noah. This likely influenced his décor for the clubs he would later own.

After high school, he entered the military and before the ink was dry on his discharge papers, he was working as a consultant to the nightclub owner in St. Louis.

To Noah, his business success story starts with The Exchequer. This was the convergence of everything he had done in his professional life, and every step in developing The Exchequer is burned in his memory.

He spotted The Barrel and knew it was the right place.

"I always thought it was a bar where biker gangs hung out," Noah said, describing the club as having great bones. A simulated barrel was the front door. The inside was surprisingly cosmopolitan; tables had inlaid backgammon games, mounted against one wall was a carved scene of a city skyline—tall and wide, this clever artwork created a three-dimensional illusion. Upstairs resembled the famous Studio 54 in New York. There was a raised deejay booth with a glass window, neon stars in the ceiling along with a hanging mirror ball, and the floor was stainless steel.

He and Sidney offered to buy the property, but the owner refused to sell it. Paul Ippolito countered with an offer to lease the building for $20,000 cash up front and $1,500 each month in rent payments. Noah and Sidney accepted those terms. New Orleans physician, Dr. Ifeanyi "Tony" Okpalobi, came through as an investor and The Exchequer had everything it needed to flourish.

From 1979 to 1981, The Exchequer hosted a variety of creative events; swimsuit contests and gong shows were crowd favorites. The Exchequer was the start of something new for Black people in New Orleans.

It was more than a plain bar with just the basics: a wooden bar counter, uncomfortable seating, and a modest dance floor. The Exchequer was sophisticated. It felt so good to Noah, he jumped at the chance to go back to that building in 1983 and reinvent it as NEXUS.

Can't you just see this as a movie?

I know just enough about production to be a great pretender. Envision the director, sweeping the room with wide-angle camera moves, capturing transformative change. In slow motion, The Exchequer logo fades out. The building, now featuring the NEXUS logo, fades up. Using high-energy music to enliven a sequence of shots, we hear McFadden & Whitehead's tune, "Ain't No Stopping Us Now," as the club is getting a facelift. The camera pans the room, revealing painters rolling a soft pastel color on the walls, floorers installing plush, deep green carpeting, an artist creating the *Sophisticated Ladies* mural, the white baby grand piano being set onto the stage; the redesign unfolds before our eyes with those opening scenes. The rebirth of 6200 Elysian Fields rebranded as NEXUS needs a movie title. How about? *From Ex to Nex* or *The Big Switch*. Since a fire had damaged the building when it was The Exchequer, what about *The Phoenix Phenomenon*?

I used that analogy to emphasize the energy Noah invested in giving NEXUS its own identity. He knew he had the right team for the renovation project when they worked thirty-six hours straight so NEXUS could open on the day he had advertised.

And when the pre-opening day arrived, the neon sign on the front of the club glowed like the sun. It was a beacon signaling that NEXUS was open for business.

This was on a Thursday. That next day, all day, people talked about NEXUS in their downtown offices, with their upscale friends, on their shotgun stoops, over the fence, in the grocery stores, at the nail salons, eating etouffee, and flipping huckabacks.

The news was hot as cayenne pepper as it spread throughout New Orleans; a new club called NEXUS had issued an open invitation to its debut.

Just like in St. Louis, when Noah reopened the revamped club there, once again, his masterful mind had created the talk of the town. Women went shopping for new outfits and men polished their best pickup lines.

When NEXUS officially opened, Noah had tracker lights sweeping the sky, limousines circling the block, and an air of excitement he had carefully orchestrated.

By 7:00 p.m. that Friday night, Noah had a packed house and a line wrapped around the building.

13

The Administrative Side of the Business

"Richard Powell's impact on NEXUS cannot be overstated," Noah said as he discussed his business partner, who, along with Noah, was co-owner and a general manager of NEXUS.

"Richard is the reason that NEXUS came into being. He invested his own money, and he brought in other investors."

The financial angel for NEXUS, Richard was away from the club for two years. When he returned, he was a quiet presence, usually in the background, keeping a watchful eye on the business.

Noah, on the other hand, was mister congeniality. He made everybody feel welcome and special. He had become an expert at running nightclubs. This was crystal clear when he talked about the mundane aspects involving The Exchequer, Noah's, and NEXUS—successful clubs with the Noah Hopkins touch. We discussed a wide range of behind-the-scenes details, including how he would choose a club location.

"I have always felt that to do a new club, you must find a building that was once a club which would mean the plumbing, electrical service, and HVAC should still be in place. This reduces your start-up costs for construction and renovations. And then, if it previously had been a club for white people, that means the majority of Black people probably had never been there and everything would be new to them."

Noah was the consummate business professional. He said attention to detail in the daytime resulted in the razzle-dazzle that occurred in the evenings. He gives credit to the team that worked with him, making NEXUS run with exceptional efficiency.

His administrative assistant, Lisa Ross, would come in around 11:00 a.m., Monday through Friday, and get the day started, checking the overnight read-outs for ten register drawers, as well as receipts paid from the cover charges at the adminission door window. She double-checked the register numbers from the previous night and also looked at the overnight list of low booze left by the operations and beverage manager, George Williams. Based on that list, Lisa would place liquor orders the following day. She was there in case people came by to repair things. She would run errands, answer the phones, schedule special event bookings, and provide naturally N'awlins warmth when responding to recorded messages.

Noah would come in about lunchtime and review forms left by the overnight managers. When the forms and cash registers came up short, the club managers were in trouble.

The same was true for the liquor inventory. George said, "If I dropped the ball on keeping track of the booze, I got chewed out and it wasn't nothing nice."

Since a lot of cash passed hands between customers and the NEXUS staff, periodically, Noah would do lie detector and voice stress tests on bartenders and waiters to make honesty their only choice.

"I paid them well, and we had high tippers. There was no reason for them to steal from me, and I did what I could to prevent employee theft."

His anti-theft measures included the installation of a high-tech Berg Dispenser System.

"This was innovative business management. We invested in this computerized liquor control system and, once again, NEXUS was ahead of the competition. I could look on the computer in my office and see a report on every pour from every bottle in the club, except wine and beer. The equipment itself, and its design, eliminated over-pouring, spillage, and theft. That's why I thought our Berg System was worth its weight in gold."

On Mondays, he would hold staff meetings with managers, the club secretary, and key bartenders to talk about what happened over the weekend, assessing what went wrong or right, keying in on anything successful enough to repeat. During those staff meetings, they also planned special events to keep the novelty edge.

Tuesdays and Wednesdays were for high maintenance; days for repairing anything broken, replacing stained carpeting, tuning the piano, deep cleaning the bar stations, and restocking low liquor inventory.

Noah could handle every single detail of the club's administrative business—he could, but he did not. He had the skills, but he also had the good sense to train and empower NEXUS managers to function as general managers. Whether it was Noah or somebody else, each day somebody prepared the work schedules for twenty-seven employees, ensured all the cash registers had sufficient money in small denominations for change, checked overhead and under-mounted lighting, and checked audio equipment downstairs and upstairs. Noah coordinated off-duty New Orleans police officers to deter criminal behavior and enforce the law. Managers interviewed bartenders, barbacks, and servers with Noah having the final say as to who got hired.

Noah was in charge of marketing and was a creative genius. He wrote his own radio spots, with the tagline "You've got that Noah Hopkins guarantee," which were produced at WYLD FM, the station where he annually spent an enormous amount of money on advertising time. He bought space on the Superdome outdoor screen. During large conventions, he would arrange to present a welcoming message to attendees and, of course, invite them all to NEXUS.

He created a VIP membership program with annual dues of $100 per person, which extended exclusive privileges to these guests. He created a monthly newsletter, mailed to all VIP members, noting members' birth dates. When they came to NEXUS on their birthday, they were elevated to super VIP status and given great perks. In the monthly members' newsletter, their birth dates were highlighted. When they arrived at NEXUS on their special day, they received a bottle of NEXUS branded champagne as a gift along with prime seating.

NEXUS had a gift shop with custom labeled merchandise, including golf shirts, brandy snifters, wine glasses, champagne and champagne glasses, windbreaker jackets, and a NEXUS branded toilet seat cover, all for a price that people gladly paid.

Elton Jones was a production manager at the TV station where I worked and I am forever grateful to him for his lighting expertise. As professional colleagues, Elton and I also had become friends. So, when he pitched the idea of a NEXUS commercial, I supported him and Noah was quick to green light the project.

Featuring a beautiful woman, you see her sensually applying lipstick. It is mesmerizing to watch her brushing her hair and then pull a silk stocking up an extended leg. The commercial cuts to this woman, stylishly dressed, getting into an expensive car she drives to NEXUS.

This was first class and unprecedented for a Black nightclub in New Orleans. It placed NEXUS in a league of its own and was submitted for an Addy award, the advertising industry's highest honor.

Don Spears worked with Noah on creative ideas, including Pot Luck Night where the craziest entertainment was presented. Customers never knew what to expect and jaws dropped at the sight of the Voodoo Snake Lady with her menagerie of snakes wrapped around her, the Master Magician who would pull off unbelievable illusions, and the ventriloquist whose lips never moved though his doll talked a lot. Every Pot Luck Night was a night to remember.

Always thinking, planning, and creating, Noah staged events at NEXUS for Mardi Gras and New Year's Eve. He scheduled the productions the week before the actual events to give the impression they were happening in real time when the shows aired on TV the day of the celebrations.

14

Wild Monday Nights

"**M**ost people think that in the nightclub business, everything happens at the end of the week—Thursday's ladies' night, Friday's happy hour, and Saturdays take care of themselves. Trust me, each of those nights takes a lot of planning and preparation and those three nights are what the majority of clubs count on to make their bottom line. But to be a super club, you have got to do more. I have always thought that if you are paying rent on the building thirty days of each month, only making money twelve days out of that month does not make sense. You must work to add at least two more days to increase your revenue."

Talking about Wild Monday Night brings back fond memories for Noah. This concept that started at The Exchequer carried over to NEXUS.

"We concentrated on adding a different twist to each of the weekend nights to keep it fresh for customers. But candidly speaking, sometimes ideas came from other sources, like Wild Monday Night."

Noah explained that most clubs accept Mondays as a dark night, but because he was open to possibilities, he stumbled onto a gold mine.

"I believe in building one night at a time. For instance, Monday, Tuesday, and Wednesday nights are challenging, but they had potential. At every Monday staff meeting, we would kick around all kinds of ideas. Everybody wanted to start with Tuesday and then Wednesday night, so we made Tuesdays a night for the Gong Show (modeled after the TV show, which was popular at that time). We did backgammon tournaments on Wednesdays. On non-holidays and Sundays, we rented to social and pleasure clubs or fraternities and sororities for events. But it was common knowledge that every club in town was closed on Mondays."

Noah recalled the staff meeting at The Exchequer, during which a bartender said he knew someone associated with one of the local radio stations, who wanted to rent the club on a Monday night. That bartender set up a meeting with Noah and Checo Yancy, who said he thought his Monday night concept could draw a crowd since every other nightclub was closed on Mondays.

"He offered $500 to rent the club on those nights. I explained to him that neither of us would make any money off a $500 rental fee. That money would not cover the cost of turning on the lights, the cost of bartenders, servers, barbacks, manager on site, deejay, plus clean up afterward. I also told him that you just don't do a Monday night without advanced marketing and advertising."

Noah felt the idea had merit since The Exchequer would be the only place open on Mondays. He also knew it would take more than one Monday because to build a night, it takes repetition, consistency, and time. Noah approved Checo's proposal as well as the significantly reduced payment of $500. For this fee, Noah agreed to turn on the lights, bring in limited staff, and schedule one manager. Since Noah had an account with WYLD, the #1 radio station in the city, he offered to handle the advertising. If the concept worked, Checo would get 10% of the door up to a capped amount. Noah embellished the idea by adding a touch of stud-power.

"I would use my friendship with Tony Elliott, a New Orleans Saints football player, to get more players to the club since they were off on Mondays. I figured the Saints would draw the girls and the girls would draw other guys. If it worked, it sounds like a wild night, so we called it Wild Monday Night."

After running a few spots on the radio and passing out flyers that first Monday night, only about sixty people showed up and The Exchequer team was nervous.

Everyone was worried, everyone except Noah. He knew it would take more than a modest radio schedule and gorilla marketing for the plan to meet projections. Willing to be patient, he had a gut feeling about Wild Monday Night. He beefed up advertising by offering the radio station 25% of the door from 7:00 p.m. to 9:00 p.m., and before long, his instincts paid off. The Exchequer had another strong, revenue-producing night.

"The second Wild Monday Night we saw close to two hundred people come through. The third Monday we had a crowd of more than three hundred fifty. After the sixth week, we were doing more than one-thousand people until finally, we were averaging one thousand six hundred people for Wild Monday Night."

Almost two years later, Wild Monday Night was re-launched at NEXUS.

"To help boost turnout, we convinced WYLD to become a co-sponsor. We also made a slight pivot and rebranded the project WYLD Monday Night, and this was a great partnership. It gave us radio spots at premium times."

From then on, NEXUS owned Monday nights.

15

The Camelot Connection

NEXUS was the right place at the right time. Young, urban Black professionals were growing in numbers and needed a place to connect; a "nexus" of social, cultural, and lifestyle factors for their generation.

Downtown was a completely different picture.

The 1984 World's Fair was a seminal point in New Orleans history. A disastrous financial flop, it is the only World's Fair to declare bankruptcy and it was the last World's Fair in the United States, which was first presented in New York in 1853.

Though they built it, people did not come, not in the droves that were needed to recapture the $350 million spent for New Orleans to host the event.

When you drive along the Mississippi Riverfront now, it is nothing like it was in 1984 when the World's Fair transformed a former railroad yard into a spectacle, featuring a monorail, gondola across the Mississippi River, aquacade, an amphitheater for concerts, the Wonderwall and the mascot, Seymore D. Fair. While the World's Fair itself was a disappointment, several old warehouses were renovated in conjunction with the event, which accelerated development of the adjacent Warehouse District.

So, as upper crust business and political leaders in New Orleans were licking their wounds, across town NEXUS was booming.

1984 was a strong year for Noah, who continued to tap into a hunger within Black people in New Orleans for an atmosphere that reflected and respected their identity. His lifelong friend, Raymond Dever, said NEXUS had a reputation that reverberated throughout the country and this was evident when sporting events were held in New Orleans.

"Major games were a bonanza for NEXUS: Bayou Classic, the Super Bowl, Saints-Atlanta, you name it, those crowds poured into NEXUS for the unofficial after-party."

What Noah did was larger than it appeared on the surface. He was riding a wave of Black economic empowerment, which paralleled a swell of Black political empowerment.

Between 1970 and 1989, about fifty cities throughout the U.S. elected Black men as mayors, including New Orleans, where Dutch Morial became the first Black mayor in 1977, a position he held for two terms through 1986.

Mayor Moon Landrieu, whose administration was a Camelot era for Black people in New Orleans preceded Dutch Morial. Landrieu empowered political groups such as BOLD, COUP, LIFE, and SOUL; groups that influenced large segments of Black voters. Lawyer-smart and streetwise, Landrieu received 99% of the Black vote on election day in 1970.

He reciprocated by hiring the first high-ranking Black officials at New Orleans City Hall, including Bob Tucker as executive assistant, Pete Sanchez, the first Black city department head, and Terrence Duvernay, Chief Administrative Officer (CAO), a powerful position in the New Orleans municipal governmental structure.

When Landrieu took office in 1970, African Americans made up 19% of city employees. By 1978, this number had risen to 43%.

This open-minded policy concerning Black employment at City Hall continued during the Morial administration, pinpointing an intersection of Noah's businesses and fair employment practices.

Many of his regular customers were employees with good-paying jobs at the city, and in the school system as well as the post office, hospitals, and offices providing medical, law, and insurance services. It is a simple principle; they worked hard all week and needed a place to unwind on the weekend. He fulfilled that social appetite in an environment specially designed for Black professionals. During the NEXUS days, they gladly paid $5 at the admission booth to cross the threshold and enjoy all the amenities NEXUS offered.

"Anybody that was anybody went there," said Carmen Baham, who started working for the City of New Orleans in 1983. "NEXUS was it for anybody in the hierarchy at the city and just like you said, it all started with Moon Landrieu. Black folks had good jobs, they were directors and there I was running the city attorney's office and we all went to NEXUS. You could go there and engage in conversations about current events, politics, world issues; we were not stoop sitters. We lived well. That was a coming of age for Black professionals in New Orleans and we loved to go to NEXUS."

Elaborating on the way she and her co-workers felt about NEXUS, she said that's all they talked about.

"At lunchtime on Thursday, we talked about getting to NEXUS for Ladies Night. And the week before we would talk about the clothes we had bought because we wanted to look our best. That's where we met up with eligible bachelors that had a little something going on professionally and financially. I know a lot of people that met their spouses there."

The City Hall connections were a blessing and a curse, as Noah would discover in later years.

But when times were good, life was better than anyone had ever imagined. And the good fortune spilled over, helping others to also thrive. Keith "Cartoonman" Douglas said Noah generously shared his platforms.

After The Exchequer opened, Noah asked Keith if he could do caricatures. It was part of the grand plan to offer a mall experience where the club would engage customers through multiple stimuli.

Keith could not answer right away.

"I had never done this kind of art before, so I said give me a week to see what I can do. I practiced and came back that next Friday and I was ready. Noah is basically responsible for me doing caricatures today."

Noah unleashed this talent, earning Keith's gratitude and admiration.

"Noah always had a great heart. He had great drive and he was an innovator. He took a chance on things that most people wouldn't try. Him being that type of visionary helped me because he saw my abilities and then had the will to help me over the hump to a new level in my career."

Keith said he blossomed as a nightclub caricaturist, but his memories involving Noah go back several years before the club connection.

"I remember when he had the Tee Top Shirt Stop; he had me cutting out film and I did a couple of jobs for him on T-shirts that I designed. Over the years, our thing just developed so when he asked me about the caricatures, it was a springboard. I'm not sure I would be where I am if I had not had that springboard."

He describes Noah as successful, yet completely unselfish.

"Noah helped so many people at his nightclubs. He definitely helped me, and he didn't ask for a dime. He just wanted me to be part of the atmosphere and just being there was good for me. The first night I made $250, charging people $5 for each caricature. He had so many customers, in just one night I did very well. Some nights weren't that good, but I never had a bad night because I was in the club just like I wanted to be, so I just partied. Seeing Noah and his ways of doing things was just wonderful."

NEXUS supported several businesses, including the caterers who served food during Happy Hour and Austin Leslie, owner of Chez Helene, who served breakfast in the wee hours of Sunday mornings following all-night partying on Saturdays.

To keep the dance music hot upstairs, he hired the best deejays, including LeBron Joseph, A.D. Berry, Slick Leo, Daryl George and Eric Sterling.

Noah said, "People ask about our secret sauce. You know what it was? Excellence—from the owners, servers, musicians, and deejays."

LeBron said the same thing in his own way.

"It was a unique set of circumstances because in addition to great owners and unlike many smaller clubs in town, NEXUS actually had a manager and an engineer as well as other structural elements that made things work. Terry Davis was a guy we'd all worked with in radio and the deejay booth was run almost like a radio station with air shifts and the like. We all took pride in knowing that we worked at the hottest club in New Orleans and did our best to keep us all at #1."

To keep the live jazz cool downstairs, Noah hired seasoned musicians and even gave young upstarts a chance to perform before a live audience. This included Harry Connick, Jr., who played piano at NEXUS when he was just fourteen years old.

At NEXUS, everyone was welcome. However, there were a few exceptions, mostly involving how people dressed.

NEXUS denied entry to Mike Edwards, a white man, but the reason had nothing to do with racial prejudice.

"No, I was certainly not turned away because of my ethnic persuasion. We were not allowed inside because we were wearing jeans. We had acquaintances who went to NEXUS and seemed to always have a good time there. But we were accustomed to bars that were more casual, so dressed in blue jeans we could not get into NEXUS."

This was not about fashion. Noah strictly adhered to rules about appearance, describing this as a psychological deterrent to bad behavior. He had a theory: when people dress well, they don't fight or act foolishly.

He led by example and always dressed impeccably. Standing six-foot-four, with a linebacker's physique, Noah is a big guy who exudes authority.

"I'm telling you it was like kissing the ring, the Pope's ring," Carmen said jokingly, adding that NEXUS had high expectations, and Noah made it easy for others to conform.

"Noah always had on beautiful clothes, beautiful shoes, and a Rolex watch. You couldn't go there looking like trash, you had to measure up to Noah. He wore nice clothes and so did everybody else. For men, that was a suit or sports jacket, some would have nice turtlenecks on. They might not have had four pennies in their pockets, but they looked like millionaires, looked like they came straight from the New Orleans Country Club."

Despite perceptions about him, Noah never forgot his roots. He remembered being an ambitious youngster with nothing and no one to lift him from poverty. Through divine intervention, he became successful. And he was always willing to help others achieve their goals. This is why he nurtured emerging entrepreneurs, including Gino Gates, who was a college student when he approached Noah with a business concept.

"I was driving down Elysian Fields the night before a holiday and noticed that NEXUS was closed. A few days later, I went and talked to Noah about booking the club on a night that I thought could be big. Skeptical, Noah said I had to pay a sizeable deposit to cover his expenses just in case nobody came. We cut a deal; I would get the door and NEXUS would keep the bar sales. When they saw how I took a slow night and packed it with about two thousand people, I never had to pay a deposit again and I was welcome to book the club the night before any holiday. I used the revenue I earned as a promoter at NEXUS to pay my way through college."

The off-duty police officers hired for NEXUS security included Farrell St. Martin, who has a lot to say about his experiences during the NEXUS days.

"Originally, I wasn't one of the first officers that worked there. It was people from the Urban Squad: Romalis Stukes, Malcolm Williams, and a couple of other guys. After Clarence Taplin and I went over to the Robbery Division, we got recruited to work the NEXUS detail and we started working there on a regular basis along with my brother, Leroy. We got to know Noah other than being a businessman and the owner of the place. He became like a big brother to us. We did our jobs, and we were always professional, but we had some fun times. We looked forward to working at NEXUS."

At first, it was easy to co-exist with Noah in New Orleans. Professionally, we were in parallel lanes. He was in business. I was in media.

But our worlds would collide when anything or anyone involved with NEXUS made the news. Sometimes the stories were positive, like when NEXUS was the barometer for Black-owned businesses thriving from tourism. Bayou Classic weekend was big. The crowds from Southern University and Grambling University had made NEXUS their post-game tradition. Reporters from all the TV stations would interview Noah about the economic impact of the Bayou Classic on his business.

Then there were occasions when the news was negative.

August 14, 1986 could have been like any other Thursday. Instead, my heart was breaking as I sat in the anchor chair, knowing the news I was about to deliver. The floor director counted backward, "Three, two, one," and pointed at me. I looked into the studio camera and read from the teleprompter.

"Good evening, our lead story tonight involves a New Orleans police detective and two police officers. They have been charged with a criminal offense in connection with the alleged unauthorized use of a stun gun. More on this story after the break."

By this time, I had become a regular among Noah's circle of friends. I knew these men, their wives, and children, and had been in their homes, watching New Orleans "Aints" football games and enjoying cookouts on Sundays.

"And we're back," shouted the floor director. Without pause, he gave the countdown, "Three, two, one," putting me and my co-anchor on alert that the newscast had resumed.

"Give me a two-shot on camera one," this command from the control room director was followed by another instruction, "Camera three, switch to a close-up of Karin."

Looking into the teleprompter, I expected to read the scripted words that made it easy for news anchors to stay with the flow of the newscast. But the teleprompter screen was black. So, I did what any seasoned professional in the anchor chair would do. I transitioned to the printed copy of the script I had been given earlier. Looking directly into camera three, which connected me to the viewing audience, I read this lead-in.

"As we said a moment ago, the New Orleans police department is investigating three of its own people, following an alleged assault on a citizen involving a stun gun. We give you the facts in this report."

With the reporter standing in front of a Wendy's restaurant, she explained, "This is where twenty-one-year-old Patrick Ledet says he experienced a nightmare at the hands of men who swore an oath to protect and serve."

As this news was being broadcast to thousands of TVs tuned to our station, I was watching, too, on the big TV monitors set up in the studio. Through the tiny earphone called an IFB tucked in my ear canal, I listened to the soundbite from the alleged victim.

"I said to my friends that I didn't know cops ate at Wendy's when they could get free food at other places. The cops overheard this and arrested me. They put me in the back of a police car where this dude kept shocking me with something in his hand. One cop laughed while it was happening. The other officer just sat there and did nothing to help me."

The story cut to a quick soundbite from a high-ranking police official and ended with the reporter describing the potential consequences for the officers. Inside the studio, the floor director shouted, "Fifteen." Five seconds later, he held up both hands, giving the ten-second signal. With just enough time to adjust my posture, I was back on camera looking at my co-anchor.

Camera two slowly zoomed in to his face, cropping me out of frame as he read from the now-functioning teleprompter.

"We must remember that these officers are presumed innocent until proven guilty in a court of law by a judge or a jury of their peers."

The switching continued with camera one now focused on me. My lips were moving as I followed the teleprompter script, but I was thinking about my friends—law enforcement officers now on the wrong side of the justice system. Those were my private thoughts. The audience couldn't see me praying that the court of divine justice would deliver mercy to my friends, followed by leniency from the court of Judge Miriam Waltzer. Viewers saw me anchoring the news, the same way I did every other day: I was in the studio, on set, doing my job.

However, concern for his friends gave Noah a bad case of indigestion. Farrell recalls what Noah did as this drama was unfolding.

"When we got in trouble with that stun gun incident, Noah came to our aid, attempting to allow us to work in plain clothes so we could still be getting revenue in. I declined because I didn't want to compound my problem by working an unauthorized detail, but I appreciated the gesture. Some people turned their backs on us but not Noah. So I'm talking about the businessman and the person. That's the best boss I ever had."

When the dust settled, Romalis entered a guilty plea. Farrell was acquitted and Tap's case ended in a mistrial. We had been friends before the case and remained friends afterward. And Noah continued hiring Farrell and Tap for police details at NEXUS. These officers knew Noah had a no-nonsense policy and anybody caught doing wrong, especially concerning drugs, was dealt with sternly.

"Any time you have a place like that and it's popular, you're not going to have a drug-free zone. Our club, and I'm saying 'our' like I owned it, but it was a part of me, and I'm telling you, NEXUS was relatively crime-free. We had some issues, but we stayed on top of them. Noah hired enough personnel, and when he had a bigger night, he hired even more officers. He did not skimp on security. NEXUS was one of the best clubs in the city. Guys who worked at other clubs, when they would finish their shifts, would come to NEXUS."

On those rare occasions when a fight happened at NEXUS, no one got hurt, though the combatants may have suffered bruised pride. That happened when long-simmering tension boiled over on a Friday night, provoking prominent real estate appraiser, Jim Thorns, to take the dispute with Melvin Rabb, an equally respected businessman, to another level.

"It was like the shootout at O.K. Corral," Jim said, as he recalled saying words that almost always end in a fight, "Let's take this outside and settle it like men."

Standing in front of the club's entrance, tension mounted. The two men went back and forth, throwing verbal jabs. And then Jim took a swing, landing a solid punch on Melvin's head. The anger intensified as the two men tussled. Dressed in expensive business suits, they fought for a few minutes until police stepped in and gave them an ultimatum.

"Stop fighting now and we'll let you both go home or if either one of you acts like you want to keep fighting, you're both going to jail."

For Jim, going home sounded like the better option, so that's what he did and Melvin did likewise.

NEXUS, under the leadership of Noah and Richard, had high standards, not only about customer conduct but also about customer service. And there was a particular employee who set the bar concerning how to treat people at NEXUS once seated.

Troy Pierre was a NEXUS server who would vigilantly watch the tables in his section. If condensation dampened a customer's napkin, Troy quickly and discreetly placed a dry napkin under the glass. If a customer's glass was empty, with the utmost courtesy, he would ask if the customer wanted another drink. He delivered this level of service consistently and people noticed.

Troy says, "Noah, Don, and Harry always complimented me on my concierge type of service…I took pride in my job. I wanted the patrons to feel comfortable. If you needed a table, we had you; we would create one if necessary."

Troy was good for NEXUS and likewise, the club was good to him. Besides being rewarded with big tips, Troy credits NEXUS for his professional development.

"NEXUS opened doors for me that I had never walked through. We had the most famous people visit us. We treated each and every guest as kings and queens."

16

Celebrity Sightings

NEXUS was already known for being an exciting nightclub and management elevated that perception to the stratosphere when Stevie Wonder visited the club, twice in the same year. Noah's good friend, Tim Francis, was CEO of Stevie Wonder's corporate empire, but before Tim took that position, he was a practicing attorney in New Orleans. The son of revered Xavier University President, Dr. Norman Francis, Tim attended a ceremony on May 18, 1986, when Xavier presented an honorary degree, written in Braille, to Stevie. During that weekend, Tim brought Stevie to NEXUS.

On July 5, 1986, Stevie was back in New Orleans for the In Square Circle Concert at the Lakefront Arena. Just so happens that Noah's birthday is July 6 and Stevie Wonder was at NEXUS to help Noah celebrate. This impromptu concert is among Noah's most special memories.

"That night was a double bonus for my customers. Sister Sledge had performed at an event at Audubon Zoo and after that gig, they came to NEXUS. With the "We Are Family" ladies singing background, Stevie performed until the wee hours of the morning. I had hired Willie T to play piano that night. He gladly gave up his seat to let Stevie stroke the keys. Stevie really is a musical genius. He made up a song right on the spot that had the club rocking."

The list of celebrities who heard about the club and knew it was something they had to experience includes Oprah Winfrey, Gladys Knight, Marla Gibbs, Whitman Mayo, Levar Burton, Isaac Hayes, and Jermaine Jackson. But Noah will always remember the phone call from Eddie Murphy, mainly because he thought it was a prank call. The conversation went like this.

"Hey, may I speak with Noah? This is Eddie Murphy."

"Who is this? I'm busy."

"No wait, this is Eddie Murphy."

And then Noah says comedian/actor did that silly laugh of his, followed by a question.

"I heard this is the place to be. Is that right?

"Yes, you heard right."

"Do you have security?"

"Yeah, we have security."

"Okay, I'll be there in about forty-five minutes."

"How many are in your party?"

"Just me and a bodyguard."

What happened next was one of the most memorable nights at NEXUS, according to Noah.

"Forty-five minutes later, a limo pulled up in front of the club and Eddie Murphy got out. I stepped outside to welcome him. He came in, went upstairs, got in the deejay booth, and clowned around for a few minutes. Then he came downstairs and got on the piano. That's when I had our photographer snap a couple of pictures of us, clowning like instant friends hanging out at NEXUS."

Eddie lucked out and came to NEXUS on a night when we had hosted a bikini contest. He and this lovely young lady had a mutual attraction.

17

The Beginning of the End

For many years, Noah tried to buy the building, and the owner steadfastly refused to sell.

Meanwhile, Noah and Richard were faithfully paying rent on a property that was falling apart. They were constantly slapped with repair costs for things like extensive termite damage that caused the wood to rot. The stability of the walls, floors, and ceilings was a constant worry for Noah.

There were also plumbing problems that gave Noah severe heartburn. He recalls one Friday night when the club was packed with customers; the band was on stage playing, and everything was going great until some pipes burst.

"All of a sudden, right over the downstairs bar, water started leaking. Customers jumped back, but they stayed. I placed buckets on the bar counter to catch the water and called a plumber who made an emergency call. He fixed the leak, but we were left with some ceiling tiles missing. We dried everything and offered to pay dry-cleaning bills for anybody whose clothes got wet, but everybody stayed and partied until about four o'clock in the morning."

Aggravations continued concerning the building and neighbors blaming NEXUS for gunfire, noise, and drugs; they even said couples were having sex in public and drunk people were urinating on their lawns.

These charges exacerbated Noah's troubles.

During this time, our respective worlds collided on several days when the neighbors' complaints escalated to news stories. As a news anchor, my scripts often included lead-ins to reports concerning NEXUS and the club's neighbors.

One evening, I attended a meeting at Our Savior Lutheran Church and School. I was there as a citizen and my presence caused quite a stir. I could hear whispers as people, who knew I was Noah's girlfriend, shared that information and suggested I was spying. For the record, I was not sent to that meeting by Noah. I went to hear firsthand what was being said and how the city councilman for that district and the New Orleans police chief would respond.

I maintained my objectivity as a journalist, even though I was not working at that moment. Talking with Noah later about the accusations, I cautioned him to brace for televised public humiliation.

The betrayals of the city councilman and police chief hurt Noah. He was also angry about the whole situation, not just because his name was being dragged through the mud, but because it cast a dark shadow over everybody associated with NEXUS, including the police officers who worked detail and his customers, who Noah believed were professionals with the highest standards of integrity. Noah had a target on his back and the weapon was character assassination.

"This all started with one woman in the neighborhood who poisoned our reputation and got everybody around her to echo her nonsense. It was a pack of lies. That politician and the police chief knew what NEXUS was about. My customers were too classy to pee outside. Why would they do that? And open sex? Never happened, not at NEXUS and not involving any of our customers."

Richard surprisingly has a different perspective. He understands the neighbor's frustrations.

"At one point, NEXUS did become a nuisance. When younger people became the predominant crowd, they didn't behave like the original NEXUS clientele. We had moved from an elitist establishment to something very different."

Disagreeing about the club's clientele was just one symptom of a relationship going sour. Richard said he and two other managers started to question whether Noah had become a liability to the club. Their suspicions became a cancer that infected the partner's relationship, leading to arguments and a toxic environment.

"I've never been the kind of person to constantly bicker and squabble," Noah said. "To me, people should look for a way to resolve conflict and since at that time, it was three or four people against me, I could not see a way to peacefully resolve what was happening."

But the demise of NEXUS did not happen overnight. It was like a slow dirge, the funeral dance of New Orleans jazz musicians on their way to the grave site for a burial.

Long before NEXUS took its last gasp, the partners agreed to expand the NEXUS brand and open a second location by securing a building on Louisiana Avenue, which became Nexus Uptown. Hoping to diversify the customer base by attracting a white clientele to the new club, they even hired a white manager.

For the 1986 Super Bowl, the iconic jazz songbird, Nancy Wilson, performed at Nexus Uptown.

Richard, Nancy Wilson, and Noah.

The plan worked for a short time but was not sustainable. Richard said, "Innate racism" reared its ugly head, which is how he explained the drop-off of white customers.

Unable to maintain the white support they had anticipated, Richard and Noah resorted to a familiar playbook. Nexus Uptown became a copycat of NEXUS on the lakefront; same format—jazz downstairs, dance music upstairs, and a racially homogeneous crowd of customers who were the same people that frequented NEXUS on the lakefront. It was as though NEXUS was competing with itself and the original club won. Richard said, "It was an expensive mistake that cost a lot of money."

Despite the disappointments, there were good times at the second location. Noah booked jazz greats Nancy Wilson, Noel Pointer, Wayne Shorter, Norman Connors and Jean Carne to perform at Nexus Uptown.

Noah got hit with another body blow when the district attorney filed criminal charges against him for alleged sales tax violations, accusing him of being too cozy with officials in the city finance department, who allegedly gave NEXUS a break from tax obligations. This time, being the preferred hangout for city officials was equated with criminal nepotism. Ordered to surrender for arrest, I remember the day he prepared to go to jail for the first time in his life.

"Should I wear dark blue or light tan?"

"I think the dark-colored suit makes more of a power statement."

We were not being frivolous. We were, instead, shielding ourselves from an intensely painful experience that was ahead. Talking about his wardrobe choice for the day was a coping mechanism that gave us a mental break before life kicked us in the gut. In a few hours, police officers would escort him to the Orleans Parish Central Lockup.

The officers allowed him to walk unrestrained, so I held his hand as we took those steps to the ugly gray building for criminals. No conversation. We were in a zone, like the night our house flooded and he faced death squarely in the face.

At those moments, the right words just didn't exist. He had been my superhero, offering his body to potential electric shock, and now I was his loyal wife, honoring my vows to stick by him for "better or worse."

My past and present converged on this day. I had climbed the ladder from production assistant to reporter/producer to news anchor. Just a few months earlier, I had quit my job at WVUE Channel 8. As a veteran in the news business, I knew what to expect.

Tipped off that Noah had agreed to surrender, the assignment editors at the TV stations dispatched news crews to capture the perp walk. Lloyd Edwards was there with the reporter assigned to him for this story. Along with a gaggle of other journalists, they recorded Noah in police custody with me by his side. The yin yang, mojo, juju—that dynamic duo chemistry Lloyd and I had enjoyed, was gone—a casualty to my career change and the legal quagmire engulfing my husband.

Charged with seventeen counts of failure to pay city and state sales taxes, Noah was booked, fingerprinted, had his mug shot taken, and locked in a small cell where he used mind over matter to transcend the discomfort.

"I meditated. I went back to the time when you and I were on the beach in Florida. I heard the waves and felt a breeze. I was at peace. If I had not treated it that way, I would have felt boxed in. I'm claustrophobic. I can't stand being in small spaces."

His time in jail was brief. Arrangements were made to get him released that same day. The case was adjudicated by Criminal Court Judge James McKay, who ordered Noah to pay $28,698.31 and placed him on five years' probation.

Noah fulfilled these terms, but harbored resentment that he took the fall. Bitter feelings were mounting. He had run the club as a solo owner from 1983 to 1985, while Richard was away for personal reasons.

When money got tight, the staff, musicians, deejays, and vendors got paid. Nagging repair bills got paid. Often, there was nothing left for Noah, and NEXUS was his only source of income.

By 1988, the pressure had grown to a boiling point. Structural and mechanical repairs carried a high price tag, which Noah could not justify paying unless he and Richard owned the building. The repairs would have been permanent improvements that would have boosted the value of the building and, ironically, given the owner grounds to raise their rent to a much higher number than the normal annual increase. So, they continued the Band-aid approach, Negro-engineering fixes as pipes burst and termite damage weakened the supports holding the building together.

The partnership was also deteriorating as people with ulterior motives drove a wedge between Richard and Noah.

Noah felt NEXUS was rotting from the inside.

At closing time on Bayou Classic weekend in November 1988, Noah implemented an exit strategy. For five years he had worked day and night at NEXUS. Two of those years required him to carry the full weight of owning the business, haggling with the building owner, and being responsible for administrative oversight. He felt entitled to a buyout, even though it fell far short of his value to NEXUS.

The next day Richard and Noah had a tense conversation.

"Did you take money from the safe?"

"I did."

"Did you deposit it in the bank?"

"No."

"Why?"

"I intend to keep what I took. You can have the club. I'm through."

The partners have different accounts of the amount of money removed from the safe. Richard said it was a large stack. Noah said it was a small amount.

"I would never have taken all the money, knowing the club still needed to operate. And let me clear the air before people pass judgment on me. NEXUS owed me and I collected a portion of that debt."

Richard said, "My saddest memories of NEXUS are when Noah and I became estranged."

NEXUS closed on December 31, 1988. Was the fatal wound self-inflicted? Were outside forces to blame? The truth is, there was no single factor. NEXUS was simply on the downside of the vicissitudes of life.

Don Spears, a former NEXUS manager, said, "A demographic shift was happening in the late 1980s. A new generation of young adults had come of age. Hip Hop became a dominant influence on music and culture. The days of class and sophistication began to wither and the original NEXUS aura started to fade."

Richard said, "A lot of nights there was almost nobody downstairs while upstairs was packed. Nobody was drinking and the bar revenue was a third of what it had been."

When NEXUS was slipping, Ladies Night was proof that the glory days were over. Richard said, "Ladies only had to pay a dollar to get in and they couldn't even afford to pay a dollar."

Noah walked away from NEXUS a few weeks before the official closing. I remember the day he came home and announced to me it was over. NEXUS was part of his past and he was ready to move forward. No sadness, no recriminations that morning, nor in the days, weeks, and months that followed.

And no answer for why it has taken over thirty years for him to unpack his memories of *The NEXUS Days*.

18

Our New Season

Ultimately, our story continues just like it began. Immersed in each other, he continues to tell the same jokes and I still laugh at them. Noah is still a creative mastermind who found a way to escape the drudgery of life during COVID-19 by taking me to wonderful jazz shows with great service and specialty cocktails. Confined to the house, our home functioned as an imaginary nightclub and we watched incredible jazz performances on YouTube. Noah was our bartender, and we enjoyed the atmosphere he had created, just like we did on October 11, 1985, the night we met at NEXUS.

That first encounter with Noah set my life on a course I never could have imagined. In 1987, we got married. That same year, I quit the news business and shortly afterwards, we formed a production company. At first, we were working at home on our kitchen table. Within three years, our company had evolved into a full-service boutique PR agency. Noah was CEO and functioned as the head of creative services. I was president, responsible for communications and public relations. Working with a team of highly skilled employees, we built an impressive client roster. But everything has its season, including that PR agency. We left New Orleans in 2004 and shifted gears, first living and working in Birmingham and later opting for a quiet life in the country.

We could chronicle our lives by the many seasons of new beginnings we have each experienced. We started life as two inner-city children on opposite sides of this country. Born into poor families, we were destined to escape our zip codes. Meeting each other was divinely ordained.

We have been together on this incredible journey. We remain best friends, have been business partners, and are truly soul mates. He is the only man who ever meant more to me than my career. I left journalism to build a life with him and never regretted that decision. He eventually left the nightclub business, also with no regrets.

6200 Elysian Fields is home to a different business now, but friendly ghosts will forever haunt that corner from *The NEXUS Days*.

After we posted pictures of NEXUS on social media in October 2020, several people shared their memories. Here's a sampling of the hundreds of comments that were posted:

NEXUS, when New Orleans was at its finest.
—**Norman Robinson**

I used to be there every Friday, like it was my job.
—Jedda Jones

Nothing but class, Noah. Part of the fabric of New Orleans.
—Rodney Cook

NEXUS was THE best nightspot in New Orleans.
—Deborah Sellers

Great folk…good music…great conversations.
—Dee Lindsey

It was more than just fun…It was a lifestyle that made us feel like we had arrived.
—Ron Thomas

Gino Gates was an advisor during the development of this book. He was also part of the NEXUS experience during the club's heyday. A world traveler, Gino said, "I went to law school in Paris. I have also traveled to other countries and I can tell you that there is nothing as nice for Black people anywhere in the world, as NEXUS."

This book is a collection of memories, a platform for people who experienced the golden years of Black nightlife in New Orleans. It is the authentic truth about the good and bad aspects of Noah's life, with NEXUS as the centerpiece.

AFTERWORD:
Reflections From Noah

As owners of NEXUS, Richard and I were the executive leaders, but many other people also contributed to the success of NEXUS.

George Williams understood how we wanted things done at NEXUS and most of the time he was on the case, especially concerning the in-house stock of liquor. I first met George when he was either eighteen or nineteen through Keith Whitehead, who was the same age. Both of them had worked at the Hilton Hotel and had a professional way of conducting themselves. Sidney and I had finished the *New Orleans Minority Business Directory* and had a reception at a club on Claiborne Avenue. We met Keith first; he was the bartender and his boss had assigned him to basically be our party planner. We were so impressed with Keith, we offered him a job at the club we were developing, which was The Exchequer. When Keith came on board, he brought George with him. We also met A.D. Berry through Keith.

By the time NEXUS opened, those guys were still in my life, though Keith had left to start his own business. Keith ran the restaurant at NEXUS and in later years, catered events at the club, including opening night. George was a trusted manager. Both Keith and George are like sons to me.

I met Don Spears before NEXUS, even before The Exchequer. I think we met during the days of Caesar's East. But we shared a love for Corvette sports cars and eventually connected as active members in a Corvette Club. Don was a manager at NEXUS who helped to sustain the club's status.

He owned a luxury car that he would park in front of the building. Don also assisted with special Thursday night events like Pot Luck, where bizarre meant better. Customers loved those nights and that concept helped NEXUS maintain its standing as a top choice among New Orleans residents and visiting tourists, including celebrities.

Lisa Ross was hired before NEXUS opened. She badgered me for a job while the building was being renovated. I liked her personality and hired her to run the office. Funny thing is, Lisa couldn't type. Despite that, she was an efficient administrative assistant and was important to the day-to-day operation of the business.

Noah Lewis was the NEXUS photographer. Any time a celebrity was at NEXUS, I could call him. It could be early in the morning; like when Eddie Murphy came to NEXUS one night about 2:30, 3:00 a.m. I called Noah Lewis and said, "Eddie Murphy is on his way here. Can you come and take some pictures?" and Noah Lewis was there just like he was for every celebrity experience at NEXUS.

Guests loved the live music sets at NEXUS and me, too. Big props to the NEXUS house band, which was smooth as silk—David Torkanowsky, Chris Severin, and Julian Garcia. Other performers included Betty Shirley, Branford Marsalis, Delfeayo Marsalis, Detroit Brooks, Donald Byrd, Ed Perkins, Ellis Marsalis, Emile Vinette, Eric Traub, George French, Germaine Bazzle, Herlin Riley, James Black, James Rivers, Juanita Brooks, Lady BJ, Phillip Manuel, Red Tyler, Victor Goines, and Wanda Rouzan.

Dexter Stephens, Ron Thomas, and Ted Burton were good friends and regular NEXUS customers who would hop on stage and imitate the Pips when Juanita Brooks sang "Midnight Train to Georgia," a tune made famous by Gladys Knight and the real Pips.

Occasionally, I would take over the microphone. My repertoire consisted of five songs. Two of them were "When Sunny Gets Blue" and "Old Folks," which I sang whenever a close friend turned a year older. People accused me of owning nightclubs so I could sing whenever I wanted to, knowing that as the boss, nobody could kick me off the stage.

The NEXUS deejays were the best in the business. Upstairs at NEXUS was jam central, thanks to LeBron Joseph, A.D. Berry, Slick Leo, Terry Davis, Daryl George, and Eric Sterling.

NEXUS was a stepping-stone for many of those guys. I have watched from the sidelines and marveled at the successful ones who have had amazing careers. The NEXUS

Air Force DJs was an incredible crew and Terry was their flight captain.

Terry Davis worked at WYLD radio while also working as a NEXUS deejay and club manager. He knew the administrative functions and like the other club managers, could be trusted to close out when the last customer left the building. Terry was usually the manager on duty on Sundays when social and pleasure clubs and other organizations booked NEXUS for special events.

There was an incredible bond between me and all the club's managers. Terry is on the special list of guys who worked with me to build the NEXUS brand.

Raymond Dever, a friend from my college years, was with me before NEXUS, during NEXUS, and after NEXUS. He is the only person, other than Jackie Yancy and Don Spears, that I let collect money at the door of the club.

Harry and Brenda Williams were close friends and regular NEXUS customers. Harry was one of my best friends. He was always there looking out for me, helping however he could. He was a reserve New Orleans police officer and acted as my personal security. When I went to the bank to make deposits, Harry was with me. Harry worked at AT&T and could troubleshoot technical problems with the phones and alarm systems at NEXUS.

Farrell St. Martin, his brother, Leroy, Romalis Stukes, and Clarence "Tap" Taplin were New Orleans police officers who regularly worked security details at the club. We became close friends, but on the job they were always the utmost professionals. Tap is the person who turned away the white guy who came to NEXUS wearing jeans. Through a strange twist of luck, we are now good friends with that man—Mike Edwards and his husband, John Wilson.

Chris Smith was in college when we first met. He came to NEXUS to ask about booking the club for his fraternity. Their event was a big success. Chris has been in my life ever since then. As a New Orleans police officer during the NEXUS days and as a professional colleague in later years, I have appreciated his loyalty and hustle. During the NEXUS days, Chris would arrange to have NEXUS promotional materials distributed inside the Superdome during major events. Fast forward to the Essence Music Festival. From 1995 through 2004, Chris was manager of operations, supervising a team of thirty people selling festival program books at the Superdome and the Morial Convention Center.

Gino Gates was a college student when we first met, and he asked to use NEXUS on slow nights. He became an attorney in the Washington, DC, area as well as a national political campaign advisor. When he talked about the impact NEXUS had on his life, Gino said, "The same way that we pushed events and parties works with candidates. I have the capacity to create geopolitical boundaries to advise clients about where to target campaign messaging, materials, and energy."

Alfred Doucette and the Johnson brothers were subcontractors who went above and beyond to get the club open. Thinking about what they did makes me appreciate them so much.

Troy Pierre was a server who was exceptional at his job. Troy had a service attitude that was personal and engaging. His tables would always have a cared-for look. That's because Troy paid attention and was proactive about his customers.

Troy Lawson is my nephew and the only relative I ever hired to work at NEXUS. He was one of the most productive bartenders on our staff and his register count was always much higher than the other bartenders. He had a huge customer following with people who wanted only him to mix their drinks.

Lawrence Gilbert would come in after NEXUS closed and clean the club from top to bottom. He shampooed carpets, mopped floors, polished brass, cleaned bathrooms, and made sure NEXUS was ready for guests. Lawrence was among the most important employees at NEXUS and is a shining example of commitment. Lawrence loved his job and always did the work with meticulous attention to detail.

I met my former partner, Richard Powell, when we were both in college. We hit some bumps in the road as partners and did not speak for thirty-two years.

When Karin tracked him down for an interview, after they talked, Richard and I had a conversation. I'm glad to report that time has healed our wounds.

I saved my final reflection for Sidney Richmond. He was not alive when NEXUS opened, but when the foundation was laid during The Exchequer days, Sidney was right there, planning and strategizing to make that club happen. He was my best friend and as young men with dreams and ambitions, we were determined to succeed. We were co-publishers of the *New Orleans Minority Business Directory*, something we did to raise money for our club project. After The Exchequer opened and was a hit with customers, we did things to sustain the business like going to hospitality trade shows, looking at and sometimes purchasing the latest equipment for hotels and nightclubs. One time when we were on a business trip in Chicago, we went to a men's clothing store. Sidney tried on a suede jacket that he fell in love with. The price tag was expensive. Thinking about his wife and children, he put it back on the rack. The next day, after packing up in my hotel room, I went to his room on a secret mission. I asked him if he had everything and he said, "Yes." I reached into his closet and said, "What about this?" It was the jacket he had admired so much in the clothing store. That's the kind of friendship we had. He died way too young, long before Karin came into my life. She only knows him through pictures taken at The Exchequer and through my stories about him. When we were writing this book, Sidney had been gone for forty years. He packed a lot of living in his short time on this earth.

EPILOGUE:
Final Comments by Karin

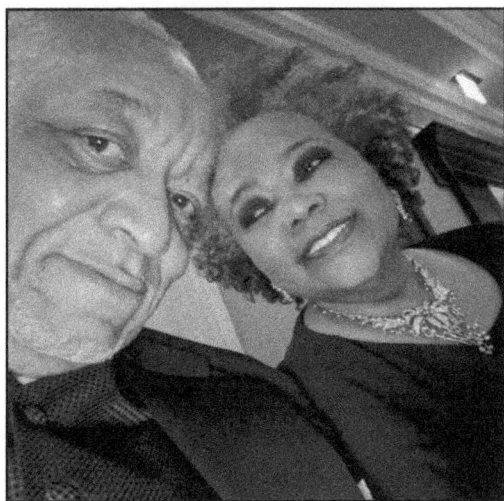

This book may be the longest love letter ever written. Calling this a love letter is my way of acknowledging that after all this time, I am still crazy about Noah. After digging into his life, I love and respect him more than ever. Admittedly, my feelings influenced my writing. However, my bias is juxtaposed to an assurance that I have been committed to accuracy and truth as I told the story of *The NEXUS Days*.

The book is a lot about Noah. After all, the title is *The NEXUS Days*. It is also a little bit about me. Since we met at NEXUS, I wanted you to get to know me and maybe even cheer for me as you read about the universe conspiring to fulfill my destiny.

I treasure my time in New Orleans, where I was fortunate to make many friends. Some friendships came from projects we worked on together, some from being in each other's company. Each one of you is precious to me. Remember when I first moved to New Orleans, the only people I knew were the doormen at my apartment building.

My New Orleans friends, you know who you are. Some of us still keep in touch. I thank all of you for embracing me, engaging me in meaningful community service, and saving me from wandering the streets of New Orleans like a lonely vagabond.

Just think about all that we did through the power of our friendships. We created a mentoring program, developed seed financing for undercapitalized businesses, developed a supplier diversity program so minorities and women could profit from maritime commerce. We wrote grants and served on boards, collaborated on a state-of-the-art production facility, and fostered world-class festivals. We cried at funerals and rejoiced at baptisms. I have a friend who was a Zulu queen and another who is a Voodoo priestess. When Noah and I lost everything to a flood, one friend bought me a new wardrobe and another friend moved out of her apartment so we could move in.

Our blessings flowed like Manna from Heaven after NEXUS.

To the staff at our former PR company: you were professionals who gave your best so our clients would shine. We were integral to the success of the Essence Music Festival, State Farm Bayou Classic, Daughters of Charity Health Centers, SWAC Championship Football Game, and many other projects.

Working together as a team in a little office with big talent, we made the impossible, possible. Thank you for the work you did, the memories we created, and the friendships that survived.

We have former clients who became friends, including a leader of the fight to save New Orleans water from takeover by a foreign company. This was not a typical PR account. Our friend and his colleagues were like David going against Goliath and the battle got rough—corporate espionage, bugging and debugging offices, even a mysterious death that escalated to suspicions of murder.

New Orleans opened my eyes and heart to unimaginable experiences and incredible friendships. Since it is impossible to name each of you, for this book, I am mentioning people I met in connection with NEXUS. The names are listed in alphabetical order: A.D. Berry, Adele Tennyson, Anne Dennis, Austin Mohr, Barbara Waiters, Bob Richardson, Brenda Williams, Brian Cain, Buster Hall, Carolyn Waiters (Carter), Charles Belonge, Chris Severin, Chris Smith, Clarence Smith, Clarence Taplin, David Eves, David Torkanowsky, Debbie Carrie (Ware), Detroit Brooks, Dexter Stephens, Don Spears,

Earl Turbinton, Emma McAboy, Eric O'Neal, Eric Sterling, Eric Waters, Erroll Quintal, Farrell St. Martin, George French, George Williams, Gino Gates, Glenda McKinley, Gregory Smith, Glynn Pichon, Henry Smith, Jackie Yancy, Jacques Morial, jai Nepal (Cordova), James Borders, Janice Manuel, Jim Hutchinson, Jim Thorns, Joe Givens, Juanita Brooks, Karen Thomas, Keith Douglas, Keith Whitehead, Kelly Netters (Key), Kevin Smith, Kurte Pellerin, Leah Weber (King), LeBron Joseph, Leroy St. Martin, Lloyd Dennis, Marc Morial, Matt Dillon, Maurice Durio, Noah Lewis, Paula Peete, Penelope Randolph, Phillip Manuel, Ray Manning, Reggie Glass, Richard Powell, Romalis Stukes, Ron Thomas, Ronnie Burns, Roy Rodney, Shirley Harmon Hopkins, Silas Lee, Slick Leo, Sterling Dourcette, Susan Eddington, Susan Taylor, Ted Burton, Terry Davis, Tim Francis, Toi Elliott, Tommy Vassel, Tony Elliott, Troy Pierre, Victor Goines, Vincent Blanson, Vincent Sylvain, Walter Ross and Wilson Willie "T" Turbinton.

To be clear, I reserved this list for people that I met at NEXUS. You made me feel welcome every time I stepped inside the club. You are the reason I stated "I felt at ease here" as I began writing Chapter 7 of this book. If you remember how we met, what we talked about and anything else that we did at NEXUS, please post your memories on our social media platforms.

In Memoriam

When I think about Rose Mary "Cookie" Rylander and Jezelle Hebert, I pray their souls have reconnected in the afterlife and fantasize that their friendship has endured. Because of these ladies, Noah and I have had the incredible life shared in this book. I tried to find Jezelle for many years to reminisce about the night she introduced me to NEXUS and Noah, but I was searching for "Giselle," which is the wrong spelling of her name. By the time I discovered the right spelling in 2015, it was too late. Jezelle had died just a few weeks before I found her on Facebook. Cookie, the friend who introduced me to Jezelle, setting the wheels in motion for me to meet Noah, is also gone. Cookie passed in 2016.

Gino Gates, wise beyond his years, was an eighteen-year-old promoter who cut a deal to use NEXUS for his events. Gino and Noah lost touch for more than thirty years, reconnecting in 2020 when I reached out to Gino about this book. He was so generous. He dipped into his data base to help me locate many of the people I wanted to interview. After I completed the manuscript, I sent a hard copy to Gino for his legal review and geo-strategic marketing guidance targeting cities throughout the country. A scheduled phone conversation was postponed when he was rushed to the hospital in December 2020. We texted back and forth for several days, sometimes about his heart condition, sometimes about lighter stuff. This volley continued until the first day of the new year when I texted, *Happy New Year* and he responded *HNY*. Though I continued texting him almost every day, I felt in my spirit that something was wrong. I had no idea why there was no response to my messages. I had no clue that communications with him was cut off forever. We opened Noah's Facebook page on January 19, 2021, and were shocked to read the many "R.I.P." posts directed to Gino Gates.

Photo Gallery

"Don't cry because it's over, smile because it happened."

— Dr. Seuss

Downstairs Bar

David, Chris and Jullian
NEXUS House Band

Natalie Cole and Noah

NEXUS
JAZZ & DISCO

DOWNSTAIRS

Marla Gibbs and House Band

Delfeayo Marsalis

Branford Marsalis

Chris Severin (left), Branford and Delfeayo Marsalis

Donald Byrd

Noah singing with Donald Byrd

Isaac Hayes   Karin Hopkins   Noah Hopkins

Juanita Brooks • Anthony Brown

George French

Wynton Marsalis and Noah

Chris Smith and Mike Tyson

Al B Sure

Noah Hopkins

Ken Norton

Jermaine Jackson

Noemi and Sister Sledge

Stevie Wonder and Sister Sledge

Stevie Wonder and Willie Tee

Jacques Morial, Sister Sledge and Marc Morial

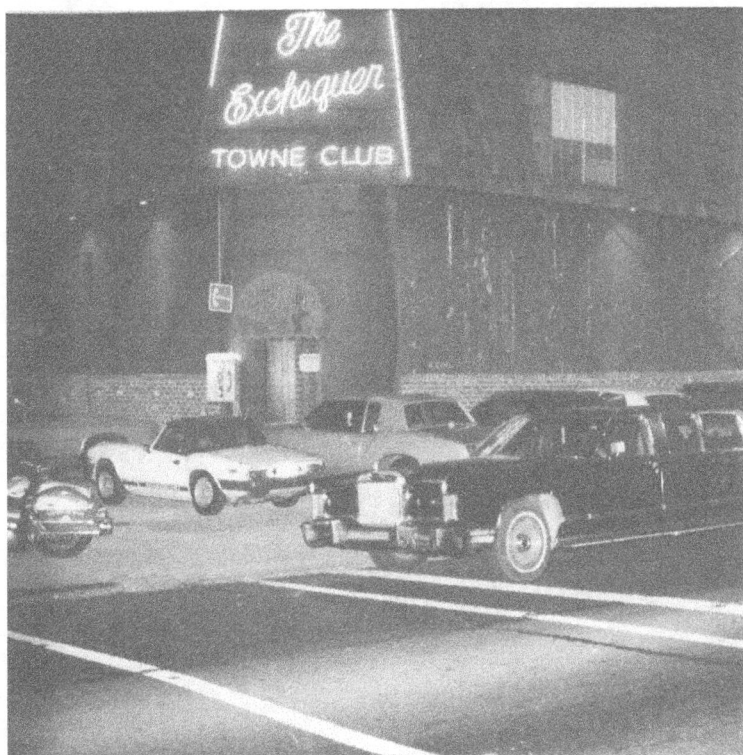

The NEXUS Days

The pictures below (circa 1979) were taken at
The Exchequer, owned by Noah and Sidney Richmond

Debbie Carrie
Kieth Whitehead
Angela Hill
at The Exchequer

Sidney Richmond   Noah Hopkins

We have been together since the day we met on October 11, 1985
We dated for 18 months and got married in Las Vegas on July 4, 1987

Acknowledgments

For inspiring me to step into this arena and believing I had a fighting chance of writing a book, I am forever indebted to Dr. Ken Mask.

Kristian Buchanan-Newman moved me from thinking about writing *The NEXUS Days* to developing a hook that got me in the writing groove.

While struggling with a title, I had a conversation with Lois Hazeur who suggested *The NEXUS Days*. This title was simple. It was right. It was it.

Several people allowed me to interview them and openly shared their memories of NEXUS. They added depth, texture, and accuracy to this story: Adele Tennyson, Chris Severin, Chris Smith, David Torkanowsky, Don Spears, Farrell St. Martin, George Williams, Gino Gates, Jim Thorns, Keith Douglas, Keith Whitehead, LeBron Joseph, Lisa Ross, Lloyd Edwards, Noah Lewis, Norman Robinson, Richard Powell, and Tim Francis. Thank you for reaching into your mental vault and pulling out the treasures that are published throughout these pages.

Amy Miller, Diane Kenney, Gee Tucker, Nora Irvine, Patricia Butts and Sally-Ann Roberts reviewed the early drafts. Each person responded with a wisdom that made this story richer and more texturized.

Special thanks to photographer Noah Lewis.

Malcolm Edgecombe designed multiple book cover concepts, including the final choice, which artistically symbolizes *The NEXUS Days*.

Speaking of art, mounted on the wall overlooking my desk are paintings that have a potent effect on me. My art is a wonderful blend of strokes and styles. My art expresses, reveals, and celebrates life. Whispering to me, these artistic muses would say, "It's time for you to use your skills as a writer to paint a picture with words."

On the practical side, I consulted with Don Spears who has written and published several books. Jerome Bailey, Tahiera Monique Brown and Jessica Tilles took *The NEXUS Days* over the finish line. They each provided consultant services concerning technical issues involved with the publication process.

Divine providence brought Jackie Adams back into our lives. She has impeccable credentials as a producer/writer in the news media. We would often cross paths with her when we were running our PR company in New Orleans. We are grateful for the times Jackie produced segments for WWL-TV featuring our clients, especially the Essence Music Festival. Now, an expert in the digital space, she owns Jackson

Squared Media. The prior history with Jackie and the easy chemistry we shared from the moment we reconnected, made it clear that she was the best person for a wide spectrum of marketing strategies, encompassing traditional and digital media.

In a funny way, my mother, Theresa Grant Mutry, also deserves credit for this book. In March 2020, this country shut down due to the coronavirus pandemic. To protect my mom, I shut down, too, rarely leaving the house and refusing to have visitors in our home. Writing this book became a welcome relief during that difficult time. Thank goodness Noah came up with creative ways to break the boredom. We took long drives with the radio tuned to our favorite Sirius satellite stations. We enjoyed jazz or R&B concerts at home, performed by artists we love whose music we found on YouTube.

I thank Noah's parents, Norah (father) and Florence (mother) Hopkins, along with our entire immediate and extended family.

Most of all, I thank God for choosing me to fulfill all of my divine assignments and enhancing my life with a husband, family, friends, and experiences that give me great joy.

"Hold fast to dreams, for if dreams die, life is a broken winged bird that cannot fly."

— Langston Hughes

About the Author

Karin Grant Hopkins is an accomplished storyteller and a first-time book author. A former television news anchor, she developed strong production skills, which she has used as a civilian to make documentaries, training films, commercials, and digital media content. Karin retired from journalism to collaborate with her husband, Noah Hopkins, on entrepreneurial opportunities.

After they established a PR company in New Orleans, she led the communications side of the business. The Essence Music Festival is among her success stories. The partnerships involved with the first Essence Music Festival were epic—*Essence* executives Ed Lewis, Clarence Smith, Susan Taylor, Karen Thomas, and Audrey Adams. George Wein, Quint Davis, and Festival Productions Inc. led production services. Karin and her team created stellar PR campaigns. That alliance attracted 142,000 patrons to the first Essence Music Festival in 1995. Festival patrons pumped $75 million into the New Orleans economy transforming the normally sluggish summer season into a tourist bonanza. She was in charge of public relations for this event for seven consecutive years. During this time frame, the Essence Music Festival experienced tremendous growth in annual attendance and economic impact.

In 2004, Karin and Noah closed their business and relocated to Birmingham, Alabama, where Karin worked for five years as Senior Public Information Officer for the Birmingham City Council.

In 2009, she was asked by the President Pro Tempore of the Alabama Senate to join his team as Communications Director where her responsibilities included liaison to The White House.

At every stage of her career, storytelling has been critical. It's how she has connected with audiences to inform, educate, and motivate them. In 2020, during a global pandemic, public outrage over social injustices, and an unprecedented presidential election, storytelling was her escape from the craziness. The result is this book, *The NEXUS Days*, which she hopes is as enlightening for you as it was therapeutic for her.

* 9 7 8 0 5 7 8 8 8 4 1 9 6 *